The Easter Party

THE EASTER PARTY

by V. Sackville-West

GREENWOOD PRESS, PUBLISHERS
WESTPORT, CONNECTICUT

The Library of Congress has catalogued this publication as follows:

Library of Congress Cataloging in Publication Data

Sackville-West, Hon. Victoria Mary, 1892-1962.
    The Easter party.

    I. Title.
[PZ3.S123Eas6] [PR6037.A35]   823'.9'12   70-139147
ISBN 0-8371-5763-3

Originally published in 1953
by Doubleday & Company, Inc.,
Garden City, New York

Reprinted with the permission
of Doubleday & Company, Inc.

First Greenwood Reprinting 1972

Library of Congress Catalogue Card Number 70-139147

ISBN 0-8371-5763-3

Printed in the United States of America

Chapter 1.

Prologue

"Walter."

"My dear?" he said, laying aside the *Times,* which she had waited for him to finish reading.

"Lucy telephoned last night. You were home so late I didn't see you and had no chance to tell you. Lucy says Robin will be back in England by the sixth. Don't you think we ought to ask her and Dick and Robin all three to Anstey for Easter?"

"By all means, my dear, if you think so. Yes, perhaps we should. We haven't seen Robin for—how long is it? Three years?"

"Four. You don't sound very enthusiastic. And truly I do hate unloading my relations on to you in this way. Have you a lot of work to do over Easter?"

"As a matter of fact, I have. As usual. But don't let that trouble you. Lucy will not take offence if I disappear into my room, will she? As for Dick, I promise to play golf one afternoon with Dick."

"One afternoon? Oh, Walter, you are incorrigible. There will be at least three afternoons. Saturday, if they arrive at teatime on the Friday; Sunday, and Monday, Bank Holiday. And what about Robin? Ought we to ask some young people to amuse him? After all, the boy has been more or less in exile all this time, four years in that remote place, and he must want a little fun."

"Young people? Noise, dancing, the wireless, the gramophone, wild expeditions in motorcars. Besides we don't know any young people."

"No," thought Rose, "we have no children of our own. So of course we do not know any young people. We are middle-aged; we have no contact with youth."

"Very well, if you'd rather not. Robin can amuse himself by catching pike in the lake instead. By the way, Juliet wants to come."

"Juliet? I thought she was on the Riviera."

"She was, but she is back. She got bored."

"Restless creature."

"But you are fond of Juliet, aren't you, Walter?"

"Oh, I adore her," he said lightly. "Is her heart broken at the moment, or is it intact, or has it found a new occupation? If so, will she want to bring the occupation with her? In any case, if Juliet is coming, remember to order some more brandy."

"You *are* unkind. Must you be going? Yes, I suppose you must. Shall you be in to dinner?"

"No. I think I told you. I have a dinner with some city company, I forget which. What about you? Are you doing anything?"

"Oh, I shall be all right. I'll ring somebody up. Don't you worry about me."

"I don't," he said gratefully; and to her surprise he came round the breakfast table to give her a brushing kiss on the top of her head. "Well, I must be off. Shall I see you this evening when I come home to change?"

"I hope so, but don't count on it. I might be out."

He nodded, picked up his brief case, and was gone. He went quickly, as always. Whatever Walter decided to do was done without delay. She heard him exchanging a few words out in the hall with old Summers, who would, she knew, be waiting there to help him on with his overcoat. Summers would reach up under the overcoat and settle the jacket into place with a couple of brisk professional jerks. He would have Walter's hat ready to hand to him. She knew it all so well, this beautifully organised life. Then she heard the front door being shut, that muted sound, and saw, through the net curtains of the dining room, the car gliding away down the street.

ॐ

"Dick."

"What?" said Dick, looking up from the *Daily Mail*.

"Isn't it nice of Rose and Walter to want us to spend Easter with them at Anstey?"

"Um."

"Don't you want to go?" said Lucy, who was easily dashed.

"Well . . . I don't mind really. Good food, good drink, plenty of comfort, nice to get into the country, and I like Rose."

"That sounds as though you didn't like Walter."

"Well, you know what I mean. I quite like Walter—admire him, respect him, and all that—but he's a bit too distinguished for me. A cold fish, I always think. And a bit of a strain to live up to."

"I do sometimes wonder what Rose feels about him."

"Haven't you ever asked her?"

"No, and I wouldn't dare."

"Your own and only sister?"

"Rose is so different from me." Lucy sighed. "I do love Rose, only her clothes always make me feel so dowdy. Isn't it odd that we should be so very different? Sisters, I mean; and you and Walter so very different; not brothers, I know, only brothers-in-law; but you did marry two sisters. I'm glad it wasn't me that married Walter," she added in her inconsequent way; "are you glad it wasn't you that married Rose?"

"If you'd married Walter making ten thousand a year instead of an unsuccessful stockbroker making five hundred, you'd have clothes like Rose and look a good deal prettier in them too, Pudding."

"Oh, Pudding, you do say sweet things to me. Not that it's true. I should never look as nice as Rose, however much money I had to spend. I haven't her chic, but I like to hear you say it. I wouldn't exchange you for Walter for all his tens of thousands. It would be nice to spend Easter alone together, just the three of us, you and me and Robin, but I suppose we had better go to Anstey," she said wistfully; "Walter can talk to Robin about the Colonial Service."

"What fun for Robin."

"Dick, we must think of Robin's future, you know. An influential uncle is not to be despised."

"Uncle by marriage."

"It comes to the same thing. Rose and I have always been fond of each other, even if we are so different, and she would use her influence with Walter if I asked her to, I know she would."

"She hasn't any influence with Walter. Nobody has."

"They say Walter could be in the Cabinet now if he liked. They say he will end up as Lord Chancellor."

Dick did not stop to enquire who *they* might be. The gossiping women with whom Lucy shared her innocuous tea parties. He said only, in a sour masculine way:

"Walter makes far too much money at the Bar as a Q.C. to bother about the Cabinet or the Woolsack."

"Dick, I never knew you were so cynical."

"Who was being cynical just now, saying that an influential uncle wasn't to be despised?"

"That wasn't cynical. Naturally I take Robin's interests. Oh, Dick, isn't it wonderful to think we shall see him again so soon? Will he have changed much, do you think? After all, he was only eighteen when he went out and he's twenty-two now. It makes a big difference. Oh, I do pity Rose and Walter for not having a son, not any children at all. I was looking at Robin's photograph, the one I have on the dressing table, and thinking how *typical* he looked, how *English*. He just couldn't be anything else, could he? I thought how those horrible natives must have *respected* him—English justice and all that. Where do you suppose he is now, at this very moment?"

"Bay of Biscay, I expect."

"Poor little Rob, I hope he isn't being seasick. He would have got his sea legs by now, though, wouldn't he? Even if it was rough in the bay? These big ships don't roll much, do they? Dick, Dick, in three days he'll be here! I declare I shall be quite shy of him. I shan't know what to say."

"I've never yet known you at a loss for something to say, Pudding. I often wonder what you do when I've gone and there's no one to chatter to. I believe you talk to the furniture while you polish it. Look, it's half-past nine."

"Yes, you must go. Here's your coat; I've mended the pocket. Nonsense, of course you must put it on, it's quite chilly this morning. Good-bye, my Pudding, good-bye, bless you, give me a kiss—oh, Dick, you shouldn't kiss me like that, not at this time of day. Good-bye, my love, see you at six; I shall be waiting for you; I might even meet you at the bus stop."

She went to the door with him and stood waving until she saw him board his bus at the corner. Still she lingered on the doorstep, liking to feel the breeze of early April ruffle her hair. There were very few people about, and she knew by sight all the cats slinking along the area railings; it was almost like looking down the street of a country town. Her heart filled with happiness; what a lucky woman she was; Robin was coming home; and she had her Dick. She did rather hope, however—though she instantly suppressed the thought as disloyal—that Dick would not call her Pudding in front of Rose and Walter. It was their little private joke, to call each other by the same name. She could not ask him not to do so; he would be dreadfully hurt; he would not understand; and she would rather endure anything than see a puzzled look come into those dear blue eyes. Twisting her wedding ring round on her finger, she thought for the millionth time how much she loved Dick, and so great a rush of love swamped her heart that, like a tide, it seemed to sweep everything into it, the April day, the prowling cats, the houses opposite, and even the bit of newspaper blowing along the street.

With a great sigh, not of sorrow but of a kind of ecstasy, she turned back to re-enter the small house. Shutting the door behind her, she paused for a moment to re-arrange the folds of Dick's lightweight overcoat hanging in the passage. He would not need it until the weather got warmer. Then she went in to the front room on the right, where they had their meals, and found their breakfast table just as they had left it: Dick's plate with a smear of jam; his knife lying across the plate; his cup with some dregs of pale coffee mixed with cigarette ash. She twirled the knob of the wireless set in the corner—they kept the wireless in here during the chilly months to save coal upstairs—and to the strains of "Housewives' Choice" tied her head up in a blue-and-white-check duster and went about her daily chores.

ह

Walter gone, Rose wondered what she should do. She ought to interview the cook, but the thought of interviewing the cook induced a small cold chill of disinclination. Every idea that came to her induced the same small droop in her impulse, a reluctance to carry out either her duty or her pleasure. She had many acquaintances; a telephone call would bring them to her house, or take her to theirs.

She would be welcome. "Darling Rose!" they would exclaim, embracing her, and then they would sit down to luncheon, unfolding their napkins as they prepared to unfold the private lives of their friends. She could easily fill her day. Meanwhile, loath to take any decision, she wandered upstairs to her own sitting room, hoping to find some inspiration there, but all she found was the cook's menu book laid ready for her inspection on the flap of her writing bureau, an ill-sharpened pencil attached to it by a length of string. *"Diner,"* she read, "smoak sammon, roas shiken, anges a sheval." She put the pencil crosswise through dinner; Walter would not be home; he had said he was dining with some city company. What about luncheon? She was offered galantine, curried eggs, and a macédoine of fruit. She put the pencil crosswise through luncheon also; she would not be in for luncheon. That, at any rate, was a decision taken. But still, what should she do?

She strolled about the pleasant, luxurious room spread with mole-grey pile carpet under Chinese rugs of coral and pale yellow. It gave her pleasure, this room; and Walter liked it. He would sometimes come up of an evening for five minutes before he went to his bath, and say what a pretty peaceful room it was; he would even sit down sometimes on her sofa and talk, although he would never lean back amongst her cushions in a comfortable way and relax. Walter always sat upright, from choice. It was an idiosyncrasy of his, and she loved him for it, as we always love the idiosyncrasies of those we love, much though they may exasperate us in other people.

Still, she had not decided what to do with her day. She

wandered about, thinking. She picked up some little jade ornaments on the mantelpiece, hoping vaguely that she might find some dust on them to blow away. There was no dust. Annie—housemaid—had done her work only too well. Rose put the ornaments down again, rearranging them ever so slightly, by half an inch—why could servants never see when things were out of symmetry? They had no eye! She felt suddenly that she hated all servants; but then she also hated all her friends and herself and everything she had to do. She even hated Walter sometimes; Walter, who, maddeningly, had her heart in his grip.

Gazing out of the window to the greening tops of the trees in the square, she wondered now why she had told him that small lie at breakfast. No, it was not a lie, it was a suppression of the truth. Why, all the same, instead of saying outright, "Lucy telephoned to say Robin was expected back on the sixth and I asked them all three to spend Easter at Anstey," had she said, "Don't you think we ought to ask them all three to Anstey for Easter," putting the responsibility of the decision on him? She knew very well that he would make no objection; he was invariably complaisant about such things. No one had more courteous manners than Walter, both in private and in public, if to have courteous manners was to accept with convincing good grace the things which bored you but which you knew to be reasonable and inevitable. Then why did she still, and always, take the roundabout way of breaking to him the arrangements she had already made?

The telephone recalled her from the window, and, transferring her cigarette in its long holder to the other hand, she lifted the receiver.

"Rose?"

"Oh, *Gilbert!*" She was really pleased. She liked Walter's brother.

"Look, Rose . . . no, it's silly to say 'look' on the telephone when you can't, isn't it? Listen, then. Are you going to be at Anstey over Easter? . . . You are? . . . Good. But have you a large, alarming party? . . . Rather large but not at all alarming? What exactly do you mean by that? . . . Your sister, her husband, their son, and Juliet Quarles. Is that the notorious Lady Quarles?"

"Well, if you call her notorious," said Rose, laughing. "She's a very old friend of ours. Walter likes her; in fact she's one of the very few women that he does like; I never can understand why. I shouldn't have thought she was at all his type. But, Gilbert, are you trying to suggest that you should come to Anstey for Easter? It seems too good to be true."

"Very kind of you to say so, Rose; I am deeply touched. That is, indeed, what I had been about to suggest. Now I feel a little doubtful. I am sure I should get on admirably with your sister, her husband, and their son—why have I never met them at your house, by the way? Do you believe in keeping family relationships neatly apart?—but I confess that the prospect of Lady Quarles somewhat daunts me."

"You need not be daunted, Gilbert; she is the most irresistible, irresponsible, loveable, charming creature on earth. . . ."

"Are you trying to tell me that Lady Quarles is cosy? If so, I don't believe it. Nothing that I have ever heard of her indicates anything of the sort. It is true that my cognisance of her is limited to the piles of illustrated papers, all out of date, which I contemplate only when I visit, in a state of the greatest apprehension, my dentist or my doctor. I am perhaps then not in the best of moods to appreciate the charm of irresistible, loveable ladies propped on a shooting stick in tweeds or entering a theatre by flashlight in an ermine cloak, but on the whole I think I had better not risk transferring my acquaintance with Lady Quarles from the printed page to the flesh. I might be disillusioned. So thank you very much all the same, I think I will not invite myself to Anstey. Besides, you wouldn't have room for me."

"Oh, Gilbert, how ridiculous you are, and how you do run on. Once you get started, nothing stops you. I see where Walter gets his loquacity: it's a family gift, I suppose, only Walter keeps it for the law courts, and you seem to turn it on at any moment, even on the telephone. You must have plenty of time to spare. I thought you were a busy man."

"I am taking a day off. Does my estimable brother never take a day off?"

"Not if he can possibly help it," said Rose. "Only when he has flu."

"What does he do then?"

"He rolls himself up into a sort of furious cocoon of bedclothes for the first three or four days so that nothing shows except a lock of grey hair on the pillow, and won't let anyone come near him, and then he emerges and sits up very uncomfortably because he won't let anyone come near him to arrange his pillows, and reads detective-story books at the rate of one every two hours."

"And it is your job to supply them? It must be like supplying an elephant with buns."

"Luckily, the supply is equal to the demand. Authors seem to have a passion for writing crime stories. I suppose it pays. Luckily also, Walter doesn't seem to mind what rubbish he reads. He just devours them, and then shies them out on to the floor."

"Where you have to pick them up. Poor Rose. What a hard life you lead. First a cocoon that won't let you come near it, and then a chrysalis that sits up in bed, and finally a butterfly that flutters off on its brilliant painted wings to the law courts, where you can't pursue it with hot-water bottles and arrowroot. By the way, how is the creature taking this paschal invasion?"

"If you mean Walter and our Easter party," said Rose, "he is bearing up well, so far. Gilbert, you *will* come, won't you? It would be a tremendous help to me if you did."

"Of course, if you put it like that . . ."

"I do put it like that."

"Rose, exquisite and charming Rose, I can refuse you nothing."

"It's settled, then. Friday afternoon? By the three-thirty from Paddington."

"Friday afternoon by the three-thirty from Paddington. Good-bye till then."

"Good-bye, Gilbert, till then."

୬

She felt better for her conversation with Gilbert; life, instead of seeming a long roll of grey drugget, took on some colour again. Energy returned to her. Dear Gilbert! With his absurd mannerisms that concealed such a good heart and so shrewd a perception of anything that might be going wrong. She was warmed by the thought of his coming; she could rely on him to float her over the dreaded moments when she saw that look in Walter's eyes meaning that he was becoming bored. Not that he ever betràyed his boredom or his impatience to other people; his trained, impeccable manners continued to function and to deceive; she alone could read the signs. He would crumble his bread, moulding the soft crumb with his long fingers into little manikins, which, Rose suspected, represented in their minute grotesque shapes the opinion that he was forming of his left- and right-hand neighbours at the table. The little crumb manikins turned into a dirty grey under this manipulation: dirty clowns he made of them. She did not want to watch Walter make bread clowns of Lucy and Dick and Robin, poor innocent Lucy and Dick and their Robin. They were her own people and she had a protective feeling towards them. Gilbert would help. Juliet would help too, with her gaiety and frivolity and charm that even Walter could not resist. With Gilbert and Juliet there the party might go well. She would have no dread of telling Walter that Gilbert was coming; she would say outright, "Walter, Gilbert rang up; he wants to come to Anstey for Easter," knowing that Walter would be pleased, for the brothers were fond of one another, in their remote way.

ह&

Stirred back into an interest in life after her conversation, Rose rang the bell. She had taken a decision at last, a decision that would affect at least one day in her aimless existence. She knew, for once, what she must do.

"Oh, Summers," she said as the old butler presented

himself in response to the bell, "is Johnson back yet from taking Sir Walter down to the law courts?"

"I do not think he can be back yet, m'lady. He would have reported his return, in case of further orders."

"When he does come back will you tell him that I want my own car brought round? I shall be going down to Anstey for the day. Sir Walter will be out for dinner. I will leave a note for him explaining that I shall not be home till late."

"What about your luncheon and dinner, my lady? Should we put up a packet of sandwiches or pack the picnic basket for you? Or should I telephone to Mrs. Whiffle at Anstey?"

Dear, motherly Summers, with his white whiskers, his extreme correctness, and his nanny ways! He tried to look after Walter and Rose and would have liked to look after them far more tenderly, had he ever dared to approach them in a more intimate way. Rose loved Summers, but Summers had no notion of this.

"Oh, Summers, what a good idea. But don't telephone to Mrs. Whiffle; it will only throw her into a fluster. I think I will take some sandwiches down with me, enough for luncheon and dinner. And a thermos of coffee perhaps? Yes, I should like a thermos of coffee, I think."

Why did she always give orders to her servants in such apologetic terms? It recalled the evasive way in which she had told Walter about Lucy and Dick and Robin coming to stay for Easter. Was she cowardly?

"And by the way, Summers . . ."

"My lady?"

"I had better tell you now in advance. We shall be

having a party at Anstey, for Easter. Sir Walter wishes it. We shall have to ask you to come down, I'm afraid, to help. We can't manage there without you."

"Very good, m'lady. Might I enquire how many guests Your Ladyship will be expecting?"

"Let me see—Sir Walter's brother, Dr. Mortibois, will be coming, and Lady Quarles, and my sister, Mrs. Packington, and of course Mr. Packington, and their son, Mr. Robin."

She watched Summers' face closely as she made these announcements, to see how he would take them. Sir Walter's brother—that went down well; that was "family." Lady Quarles—Summers blinked, but recovered himself quickly; it was evident that he could not entirely approve of Juliet, but consented to accept her as a family friend, and a very openhanded one at that, wildly generous tips all round on leaving and certainly what he would call a real lady, in spite of her little failings at the cocktail bar and in the divorce court, all well known and enjoyed in the servants' hall. Summers, who had slightly lost his balance at the mention of Lady Quarles, tottering momentarily on his old legs, recovered it when Mrs. and Mr. Packington, Lucy and Dick, swam up like large, respectable fish into the picture; they were "family" too, albeit her ladyship's family, not Sir Walter's, and thus a little lower in the social scale: not quite on the same level, but still family and thus to be accepted. So far, Summers had taken everything well, decorously, deferentially, dutifully. But at the mention of Robin's name, at the end of the list, a light of real pleasure gleamed in the faded eyes.

"Mr. Robin, my lady? It will be nice for you and Sir

Walter to see him home. And for Mr. and Mrs. Packington too. I am sure that everyone at Anstey will be glad to welcome Mr. Robin. I am sure that for my own part I will be glad to welcome him. . . . Now if you will excuse me, my lady, I will go and see if Johnson has reported back, when I will instruct him to bring round the car. The menu book? Should I take it? If Your Ladyship would kindly write a note ordering the sandwiches and the thermos of coffee . . . The kitchen never likes taking orders from the pantry. . . . Thank you, my lady."

Summers bowed himself out, the Lord Chamberlain retiring backwards before the Queen.

ॐ

Rose was glad she had decided to spend the day in the country. A little smile hovered round her lips: Gilbert and Summers between them had managed to make her feel quite cheerful. She must leave a note for Walter. Supposing she wrote, "Dear Walter. You will not find me here when you come in, I am leaving you forever." How much would he mind?

"Darling," she wrote, "it is such a lovely spring day, I thought I would go and spend it at Anstey. Besides, I must see to housekeeping things down there, if we are going to have all those people for Easter. Gilbert is coming too; he rang up. Shan't be back till after dinner. Love, R. P.S. Sorry to miss you. I will give your love to Svend."

ॐ

The car turned off the main road after the long run down between the Buckinghamshire beech clumps, very rounded and noble on the sky line, still black and leafless in this early April day. Rose had enjoyed the run, driving fast. She always drove fast; too fast, taking risks. This road, if she pursued it far enough, would take her right down into the depths of England, right down into Gloucestershire and Hereford and into Wales, until she came to the outer edge of the island and ran off it, smashing the car and herself to bits off some rough cliffs into the breakers of the Atlantic. She dwelt for a moment on the idea, amused at her own imaginings, knowing that she would never find the courage to carry them out, any more than she would ever find the courage to tell Walter that she wanted to leave him forever.

These were things that she would never do.

Meanwhile the car rolled obediently down the length of the private road leading to Anstey, down the gravel lane, crunching millions of biscuits under the tyres. Walter had to keep this road in repair at his own expense; he had spent a thousand pounds on it last year, a thousand pounds he could well afford. Walter could afford anything; his wife, his house, his road; as by his own personality he could without conscious effort impose himself on other people, to his own liking, not necessarily to theirs. They had to accept him as he intended himself to be.

ଽ�

Anstey came into view at a turn of the lane. Rose dropped her speed from thirty to twenty, to take a slow look at her home. She looked at it as though she had never seen it before. A curious experience! There it was, just as she remembered it and knew it so well: very demure, of rosy

Queen Anne brick, set in its park of great trees. *"How typical,"* she thought, *"how English!* It just couldn't be anything else, could it?" She had a sudden rush of love to her heart for it, unexpected. She changed gear and drove on, sweeping up to the base of the steps that led in a double flight to the front door.

No one had heard her arrive. She was glad about this because it meant that she could steal away, unobserved, for a walk in the garden before she need make her presence known. The windows on the front were all shuttered, giving the house a blind look. The only living creature that had so far observed her arrival was Svend, the Alsatian. He lay sunning himself at the top of the steps, a guard, waiting. Rose knew that he would wait there indefinitely until Walter should choose to return. He lay with his paws crossed in pale elegance, dangling over the edge of the step. What natural beauty the dog had! No sculptor could have placed him better. But a sculptor would have hardened him into a thing of stone or plaster or marble, not this soft deep living thing of fur and muscle and bone, so young, so eager, so warm, with so black and moist a nose. Such golden eyes, such alert and pricking ears . . . He pricked them straighter as he heard the car coming; arose with enormous dignity; stretched himself; yawned; and descended the steps to greet his guest.

The son of the house: the young host; the courteous young host.

Rose got out of the car.

"Hullo, Svend," she said, putting her hand in a perfunctory caress on his head. "Waiting, as usual? Sorry I haven't brought Walter with me. Let's go for a walk all the same, shall we?"

Svend was only too pleased. He responded at once. He galloped away ahead of Rose, gambolling down the paths; galloping back towards her, gambolling in wide circles across the grass. He raced about, he tore about, inventing little games for himself, tossing bits of stick up into the air, catching them, throwing them again, inviting Rose to throw them for him. He went all wildly gay, and Rose too went almost gay in this truant hour when only Svend knew that she was there. They were happy together, quite simply, with no complications, both of them so forgetful as to forget even Walter, just enjoying themselves in the big expanse of Anstey, the great green grass slopes going down towards the lake.

ह∾

The beauty of the renowned Anstey gardens! Rose stood amazed. Svend brought one of his little sticks and dropped it at her feet and stood looking up, waiting for her to throw it, but she could take no notice. She was gazing across the lake, with the great amphitheatre of trees piling up behind it, and the classical temples standing at intervals along its shores. It was one of the most famous landscape gardens in England, laid out in the eighteenth century, far too big for the house it belonged to. The house, however, was not visible from here, and, but for the temples, the garden might not have been a thing of artifice at all, but part of the natural scenery of woods and water, stretching away indefinitely into the countryside, untended by the hand of man. Already the legions of wild daffodils were yellowing the grassy slopes, and a flight of duck rose from the lake, which they frequented of their own accord. The deep re-

flections of willow and silver birch quivered slightly, then
resumed their immobility. The air was soft with the first
warmth of spring, which is so different from the last
warmth of autumn—the difference between the beginning
and the end, between arrival and departure. Rose, not particularly sensitive to the beauties of Nature, was bound to
recognise that this was a very lovely spot on a very lovely
day. Walter was a lucky man. So any observer would think
who could have this vision of Walter's possessions at that
moment—his romantic estate, his graceful wife, his handsome dog.

"I do hope it will be fine for Easter," thought Rose, not
only because her social instincts readily came to the surface, but also because she was a little apprehensive about
this party.

Turning, she strolled back up towards the house. It was
still there, pink and cream. The shutters had been opened
and the blinds drawn up; no doubt Mrs. Whiffle had seen
the car standing at the front door. Rose sighed. Her little
interlude was over. Now there would be bustle and ex-
clamations. For one moment she paused, still unperceived,
having Anstey to herself. It looked so quiet and empty, as
though it were thinking things over, knowing that within a
week it would be noisy with life. Houses, some houses,
seem to know what is going on. It is their fate to be compelled to contain whatever they are asked to contain,
whether happiness or trouble, but the hour passes and the
silence returns.

"My home," Rose said aloud. "My home," she repeated.
The words meant nothing to her. "It isn't my home," she
said; "it's nobody's home." A nesting bird had dropped a

trail of straw on the clipped box edging; she removed it irritably—it looked untidy—yet she envied the nesting bird. "Svend!" she called, and he came in instant, anxious obedience, sitting down on his haunches in front of her, to learn her pleasure. He was so tall that she could reach his head without stooping, and gave his ear so sharp a tweak that, in surprise, he uttered a whimper of pain. "It's *your* home anyway, isn't it?" she said. "The only home you ever knew since you were a puppy and couldn't go up or down stairs by yourself and Walter had to carry you. You would be perfectly happy here alone together, Walter and you, wouldn't you, Svend, without me? Come on now. *Heel.*"

He followed her close at heel, contrite, aware that things had changed, and that he was in disgrace.

Chapter 2.

FRIDAY EVENING

"Juliet has missed her train."

"What else did you expect?" said Walter, who for once was sunk into the depths of an armchair, Svend lying beside him. They were all having tea in the hall, near the blazing fire which Summers had lighted, although the weather was as fine and warm as Rose had hoped. Lucy looked up, appalled. She and Dick never missed trains.

"She has changed her mind now and is coming by car. Her own car has something the matter with it, so she has got somebody else to drive her down."

"Meanwhile, I suppose Johnson has gone to meet her at the station."

"Oh yes, of course he has. It would never occur to Juliet

to telephone at once, in time for us to stop him. I expect she was busy fixing up with the somebody else."

"I don't believe it," said Walter. "She never meant to catch that train; there is nothing wrong with her car; things don't go wrong with Rolls-Royces; she always meant to come with Mr. Somebody Else, with whom she has no doubt been spending a delightful afternoon."

Lucy gave a gasp.

"What did you say, Lucy?"

"I didn't say anything, Rose, nothing at all. I was just thinking, isn't it a little inconsiderate of your friend?"

"Wait till you see Juliet," said Walter. He got up, putting his cup back on the tea table. "What a nice evening. Come down for a stroll to the lake, Gilbert?"

Svend got up too and followed, his nails clicking on the polished floor. The sound was muted, at odd little intervals, as he crossed the Persian rugs with which the floor was strewn.

ક્ર

Rose, left alone with her own relations, realised that she must pull herself together and display affection. She must establish an atmosphere of security which would enable Lucy, at any rate, to face Walter and Anstey without too much twittering. Dick could look after himself; it would take something more than Walter to wobble his male solidity. The boy Robin she was not so sure about, not having had time to observe him; she remembered him as the callow nephew of eighteen, four years ago, into whose hand one could still dare to slip a tip of a treasury note on parting—"Oh, I say, thanks, Aunt Rose, thanks awfully"—

but who now confronted her as a grown-up young man of
twenty-two, having acquired a certain poise, an assurance
of manner which she, as a woman of the world, suspected
of being somewhat precarious. He was undoubtedly very
good-looking, in the obvious way that many young English-
men are good-looking: crisp and clean and fair, wearing
his clothes well—he would not disgrace the pervading elegance of Anstey; as a nephew he was most presentable.
What he was like inside remained to be discovered. Perhaps there was nothing inside, beyond a conventional
decency of behaviour and a few little mice of gay dissipa-
tion scuttling harmlessly behind the wainscot.

There they were, so closely bound in their trinity, the
family, her own family, and she must cope with them,
protect them.

She went and sat on the arm of Lucy's chair, putting
her arm round her sister's shoulders. In the other hand she
held her constant cigarette in the long holder, stretching
it away from her so that the smoke should not blow back
into Lucy's eyes. Even into this gesture she contrived to
put the fluent grace that Lucy envied. Lucy looked down at
the dangling foot, the slim silk ankle, the crocodile shoe.

"Dear Rosie!" she said comfortably.

"Darling Luce, it is so lovely to have you here, all three
of you, and perhaps specially Robin. Do you remember,
Robin, how you used to come sometimes in the summer
holidays? What fun we had with the boat on the lake!
And that time when you were bathing and got frightened
by a swan? It swam right up to you and you thought it
was going to peck your nose off. You screamed and
screamed. I simply long to hear all about your adventures.

How nice to think it is only Friday and we have got until Tuesday, plenty of time. Now what would you all like to do? Stay in here? Go out? I ought not to go too far in case Juliet arrives. When I took the message I quite forgot to ask what time she had left London."

"Does she always behave like this?" said Lucy, interested in Lady Quarles, whose photograph she had seen in *The Tatler* when she went to the hairdresser.

"Always. She is said to have missed the Golden Arrow every day for a week, only of course nobody ever knew what was keeping her in Paris."

"Oh," said Lucy, shocked, but more fascinated than shocked.

"You beware of this siren, Robin," said Rose, hating herself for her bantering tone, but feeling that it was something the Packington family could understand. "And you too, Dick. There's no harm in Juliet really, but it is an axiom that no man should consider himself safe from her."

"Ha!" said Dick, rather like a horse neighing. Rose, who expected to see steam coming out of his nostrils, was unable to interpret the exact implications of this exclamation; it seemed fruitless to enquire. And as it was practically the first remark that Dick had made since entering Anstey, she must not discourage him.

"Robin, ring the bell; we'll get tea cleared away. I'm afraid," she continued, addressing nobody in particular, "the drawing room is all shut up, so we have to pig it in here." Lucy looked round the pine-panelled hall, with its crackling fire, big sofas, deep chairs, and central table strewn with illustrated papers, flowers everywhere, great branches of golden forsythia springing from urns in cor-

ners, so tall and lavish that they might well have been
growing in the garden instead of picked for indoors, great
bowls of daffodils dumped on whatever table would take
them. All the light-coloured flowers of April . . . and
now this old stage butler of a Summers clearing away the
tea-things with such quick and quiet efficiency. Such care-
less luxury did not correspond at all to Lucy's idea of
pigging it.

Looking round at the prodigality of flowers, Lucy, who
allowed herself two shillings a week out of the housekeeping money to buy a bunch of anemones for the dining-room
table, thought that Rose might really send her a few flowers
sometimes. Still, Rose's arm was very affectionately round
her shoulders, giving her a sisterly warmth, and Rose was
certainly being very nice to Dick and Robin.

"I say, Pudding," said Dick suddenly.

Lucy jumped.

"Yes, Pudding darling, what?"

"Nice dog, that of Walter's. Sort of Rin Tin Tin. You
remember Rin Tin Tin on the pictures?"

"You're quite right, Dick," said Rose, thankfully grasp-
ing this new and fruitful topic. The Dicks of English life
could be depended upon to talk dogs for as long as one
could encourage them to do so. "How clever of you, Dick,"
she said, "to notice so quickly. Svend is quite an exceptional dog. And so beautiful, don't you think? Like a piece
of sculpture, sometimes, the way he lies; he seems to have
an instinct for arranging himself in perfect lines. Or like
a Chinese drawing of a deer, legs folded, nose curled
round . . ." She saw she was getting out of Dick's depth,
and desisted. "Yes, he's a very clever dog," she ended

lamely. "You're quite right, Dick: a sort of Rin Tin Tin. He ought to be a film dog. Only, you see, he's Walter's dog, and Walter would never let him go either to Denham or to Hollywood."

"Well, I don't know so much about Denham or Hollywood," said Dick, whose power of speech seemed suddenly to be released; "all I can say is that when he lies on his back, with all his paws in the air, he reminds me of a photograph I once saw, a picture postcard, I think it was, of a dog that had been found after hundreds of years, buried in lava, or ashes, or something, by a volcano. Horrible, it was. All twisted and crooked, poor brute, as though he'd seen death coming and tried to escape from it. I wouldn't be surprised if Svend ended up something like that."

These unexpected remarks produced a blank of dismay. Robin was the first to recover himself.

"You mean the Pompeian dog, Daddy," he said. "I sent you the postcard myself, from Naples. It seems to have made an impression."

"You shouldn't have sent it, Robin," said Lucy with a shudder; "I burnt it at once, but we've never forgotten it. You should have sent a nice view of Naples instead."

"Anyhow, Dick," said Rose, cheerful again, "for goodness' sake, don't go telling Walter about it. He cares for that dog more than for anything on earth, I do believe."

"Except for you, Rosie," said loyal Lucy.

"Oh, far more than for me—— Yes, Summers, what is it?"

"If Annie might have Mrs. Packington's keys, my lady."

"Oh, *please* tell Annie not to bother," said Lucy in a panic. She knew how often she had darned Dick's pyjamas and her own nightgown. "I'll unpack myself, presently. It won't take me a minute, and I'm sure Annie has more than enough to do." She smiled ingratiatingly at Summers, who failed to respond.

"Very good, madam. As you wish."

ॐ

Rose, aware that this family conversation was going rather stickily, not at all as she had intended it to go, got up, stubbing her cigarette into an ash tray. Perhaps it would be better if she got Lucy away to herself.

"Well, Lucy, if you refuse to let Annie unpack for you, shall I take you up to your room? Dick and Robin will be quite happy down here, won't you both? Summers will bring the drinks in a few minutes." This was one of her oblique orders to Summers; she could avoid addressing him directly; she knew that he would be listening, for he was still there, making up the fire, his plump black bottom in its pin-striped trousers humbly bending. "Come on, Luce, let's leave them to themselves. We shall hear from upstairs when Juliet arrives."

"Dear me, aren't you extravagant," said Lucy, preparing to follow her sister, "wasting half a cigarette like that! Now if I caught Dick doing such a thing . . ."

"You would tell him off?"

Rose glanced at Dick; he was grinning; evidently the understanding between these two was very close and fond. Private jokes between married people with years of daily intimacy between them . . .

"Wouldn't you tell Walter off?"

Rose laughed in real amusement.

"Walter could hurl a whole box of cigarettes into a bon-fire and I wouldn't say a word. But I like being scolded by you, Lucy; it takes me back to our nursery days." She put her arm through her sister's as they went upstairs. "Darling Luce, you don't know how happy I am to have you here."

"Really and truly, Rose? Do you know I was rather frightened about coming. I am so terribly afraid of boring Walter—and of course his brother. You didn't tell me he would be here. One knows about him as the great brain specialist, of course; he is terribly eminent; one sees his name in the papers, but I never thought I should meet him in your house."

"Gilbert? Oh, did I forget to tell you he was coming?" She had not forgotten; she had simply committed another one of her evasions. "You mustn't be alarmed by him, he is the easiest person."

"But he must know everything that is going on inside one's mind," said Lucy in one of her moments of somewhat muddled perception.

"Does that matter? Is there anything inside *your* mind that you wouldn't like him to know?"

"Isn't there something, sometimes, in *all* our minds?" said Lucy, pausing on the landing as she might pause in alarm before a new discovery.

ક્ર

"Here is your room," said Rose, shutting the door behind them. "I do hope you will be comfortable. It is the room you have always had, so you will know your way about the cupboards and so forth. Dick has the room next to you— the dressing room—and Robin has a poky little room just opposite, on the other side of the passage. You will all three have to share a bathroom—I hope you won't mind."

"Oh, Rosie!" said Lucy, suddenly hugging her. "Really, you are the simplest, sweetest person still, in some ways. How can you imagine that I should mind sharing a bathroom with Dick and Robin? How do you imagine we live in Ontibon Street? Do you think we have a bathroom each? You show me into this lovely room and then seem to apologise for it. Bath salts in the bathroom too. Goodness, Rose, don't you realise the difference between your life and mine? Oh, I ought not to say that," said Lucy, who had determined not to say it, but whose natural honesty got the better of her. "Still, we *are* sisters, and if I can't be truthful with you, who can I be truthful with? We've always known the worst of each other; I suppose that is what sisters are meant for. . . . Do you remember how you used to rub the soap in my eyes when we were having our bath? I think perhaps you were born to rub soap into my eyes and make them smart."

"Oh no, Lucy, no!" said Rose, overcome by remorse. "Surely not!"

"Well, I dunno," said Lucy. "I don't bear you any grudge for it. You were born for success, I daresay, and I wasn't. Anyhow, I'm happy," she said defiantly, "and that's more than most people seem to get from life."

"You must be very happy to have Robin home. He's a very nice-looking boy, your Robin."

"Oh, Rosie!" Lucy became emotional. "Oh, Rosie, you don't know what it means to us, Dick and me, having Robin back. Before he arrived we said to each other what a pity it was that you and Walter hadn't any children. . . .

Oh dear, I oughtn't to have said that either," said Lucy. "Sorry, Rose, if I've said the wrong thing. Only you and me being up here alone together makes me talk to you as though we were still having our bath, and then our glass of milk and our biscuits for supper—do you remember?"

"Yes, I remember," said Rose; "shall I ever forget? Very dry and nasty they were, too. And that glass of milk, leaving smears of our mouths round the rim . . . I always hated that. Afterwards, in our twin beds, I used to go to sleep thinking about it till I was nearly sick into my pillow. You never knew that. Isn't it odd, the way one minds about things, and keeps it all to oneself, and never thinks to tell it even to one's nearest and dearest—because I suppose, Lucy, you were my nearest and dearest in those days, weren't you?"

"There was only us two," said Lucy, "except for Mummy and Daddy. We could have told each other anything. There were no husbands in those days," she said, on the assumption that husbands were all-important. She was on the point of adding, "and no sons," but bit it off her tongue in time.

"We squabbled," said Rose. These reminiscences with Lucy were, as always, giving her a great deal of pleasurable pain. It did not seem to matter how often they went over the same ground. "We squabbled a lot, you and I."

"Oh, we *did*," said Lucy with enthusiasm. Even squabbles turn into romance in retrospect. "Don't you remember how you picked the eyes out of my doll and threw them on the fire? You said they were like boot buttons and you couldn't endure them. I expect you were right. You always had better taste than I had. How I yelled! Mummy rushed in, thinking I was being murdered."

"They were awful eyes," said Rose, remembering. "Hard. They stared."

"And then there was the other time," said Lucy, babbling on, "when we had a tug-of-war over my Teddy bear. You said you didn't like Teddy bears: they were too smug and soft and cosy. So between us we pulled him to pieces and there was nothing left but a lot of sawdust all over the floor. I minded about that; I remember I howled. I didn't like you destroying my Teddy bear. Why did you, Rosie? It wasn't kind. It was cruel of you."

"I'm sorry," said Rose, thinking that if Walter set himself to pull Lucy's Dick to pieces he, also, would leave nothing but a lot of sawdust all over the floor. "I'm sorry, Luce; I shouldn't have done that. One should never destroy a person's Teddy bear. It isn't kind; it is cruel; it is unnecessary. . . . Do you know, Lucy, you are the only person in the world who still calls me Rosie?"

"Mummy and Daddy used to."

A short silence fell between the sisters; then Lucy resumed:

"Rose? You didn't really mean that, did you, about Walter and Svend? I mean, about Walter being fonder of a dog than of you?"

"Of course not; I was only joking. . . . All the same," said Rose, "there certainly is a very strong bond between those two; a sort of affinity, if you understand."

"They say that dogs do get to be like the person they belong to," said Lucy, trotting out one of her stereotyped little phrases. "Even physically, not only in character. Walter and Svend have both got the same broad forehead. And," she said, pursuing her discoveries, "they are both very grave and dignified, aren't they?—with a kind of reserve, rather forbidding, though you feel that they are quite gentle underneath. You feel sure that Svend wouldn't hurt a flea, even if he had one."

"I doubt if the legal profession would say as much for Walter," said Rose, amused; "he is pretty formidable once he gets going. The wretched little insects he has in the witness box don't stand much chance against him; but Svend doesn't have fleas," she added. "No dog of Walter's would ever dare to have even the smallest flea."

"No, you certainly do live in a grand way," said Lucy, taking a short cut in thought and looking round her with a sigh. "Anstey makes Ontibon Street look terribly huggermugger." Her nature was far too honest for petty suppressions of envy. What she felt came out. "Rose, don't you ever feel alarmed by all your grandeur? We weren't brought up to this sort of thing, you and I. Remember the Rectory, when we thought ourselves lucky if we could afford a woman to scrub once a week? Summers, for instance, he frightens me out of my life."

"Would it interest you to know that Summers is a Communist?" said Rose, blowing a ring of smoke from her cigarette and spearing it with her finger before it dissolved in the air.

"*What?*" said Lucy. Rose could not have startled her more by indicating that Summers was the devil dressed in bright scarlet.

"Oh yes," said Rose easily; "I found that out long ago.

He happens to be devoted to me and Walter, and to have all the correct reactions about class and family and friends and so on, but he flies the Red Flag by conviction all the same. I often think that Summers must be a very unhappy man. Torn between his instincts and his political principles. A division of loyalties."

"But, Rosie, he might *murder* you."

"I don't think we are in much peril. Svend might bite him, if he laid hands on Walter, and he wouldn't at all like to be bitten by Svend. Nor should I. Those great white fangs tearing into one's flesh—— Not that Svend would ever bite *me*; he accepts me as an appendage to Walter. One of Walter's chattels. He would no more think of savaging the curtains in the hall than of savaging me. . . . All the same, Lucy," said Rose, a sudden terror coming into her eyes, "supposing Svend or Summers did turn on me someday? One lives among danger, doesn't one? One never knows whence it will come. One shouldn't think so much, should one, Luce? It is better not to think. One must just live from day to day. One should have been born a bit tougher, that's all. I don't think Summers' Communism goes very deep. And in any case, if I were Summers, I should certainly share his views."

"Rose!" said Lucy, appalled by this heresy. It was as though Rose had proclaimed her intention of not going to church on Easter Day.

"Well, of course I should. . . . However, don't let us argue about that. Let us just be happy while we may. I do hope you will be comfortable, Luce. I wasn't sure," she said diffidently, "if you and Dick still liked to share a room or not. You can suit yourselves. There is a double bed in

here, but there is also the dressing room for Dick next door
with a bed in it, if he prefers to use that."

"Oh, Rosie, Dick and I always sleep together. He says he
would feel lonely if we didn't."

"And how about you, Lucy? Would you feel lonely?"

"Well, Dick does snore. And I don't sleep very well.
Sometimes I would like to turn on the light and read for a
bit, but that might wake him, so I don't. I don't read very
much anyway," said Lucy truthfully; "there never seems to
be time. But I do like the picture papers and I saw you had
a lovely lot on the table in the hall—*Vogue* and *The Illustrated London News*, and *Country Life*, and *The Tatler*
and *Punch*—I do love *Punch*, don't you? *Picture Post* is the
only picture paper we can afford at home. Fourpence a
week." She said this in no complaining spirit, but as a mere
statement of fact. "I think I'll give a miss to some of the
papers you have here," she said with a little giggle; "*The
New Statesman*, and *The Spectator*, and *The Economist*,
and *The Burlington*. Dick and I aren't high-brows, you
know."

"Yes, I know," said Rose, knowing only too well. Living
in the rarefied atmosphere of Walter had unfitted her for
this sisterly chatter. She was beginning to feel it should be
brought to an end, but could see that Lucy was fairly set
for a long sail. She fretted for an interruption. It came.

"My God," she said, hearing a commotion downstairs,
"that must be Juliet arriving. We must go down and rescue
Dick and Robin—or would you rather stay up here and
unpack?"

"No, I'll come," said Lucy. She was pained by Rose
saying "My God," and she longed to unpack, but she was

full of curiosity to see Juliet Quarles. Having entered this rakish wolfish den of Anstey, she might as well make the most of it.

ह∞

"Dar-*lings!*" said Juliet, bursting into the hall in a swirl of furs and scent. "Oh, my sweets, I do apologise, I grovel. I——" She came to an abrupt end, seeing that the people in the hall were not any of her sweets or darlings, but two unknown men of differing ages. "Oh," she said, "where are Rose and Walter? I'm terribly late. I missed my train. I hope they got my message. I tried to ring up myself, but all I got was the engaged signal bleating like an old sheep, so I had to start, leaving it to my idiot of a maid to get through when she could. . . . Look, I don't know who you both are, except that you must be Rose's brother-in-law and Rose's nephew. She told me you would both be here for Easter; she told me how excited she was to see her nephew again. Robin, isn't it? Yes: Robin who had been away on some ghastly job in some ghastly place for four years. That's it! That must be you. And you must be Dick," she said, swirling round towards Dick. "Rose has told me so much about you; I've always longed to meet you. Darling Rose! what a wonderful sister-in-law to have! But where is she? And where's Walter? Gone down to the lake, I suppose. . . . Oh, Bobby, you shouldn't lug in all that luggage. Put it down. Summers will see to it. This is Bobby," she explained, waving her hand towards a young man in Air Force blue, carrying a large rawhide Revelation suitcase in either hand. "Bobby, my love, if you're going to make a practice of carrying my luggage I must buy you a yoke, like a dairymaid, you know, with a bucket dangling on each end—— Oh, Summers, there you are. How are you? How's your rheumatism? Have you ever tried Sloan's liniment? You must *dab* it on; don't *rub* it in, or it might give you spots. Look, Summers, there's my luggage: could you get it taken up to my room? No, wait. It's too heavy for you alone. Lord Robert will help you. You will, Bobby, won't you? And here are my keys. Annie will unpack for me, won't she? I never can see the sense of locking things up in England, can you? We were supposed to be such honest people, weren't we? But perhaps things have changed. Anyhow, here are my keys, take them, Summers, will you? And how is Annie?"

"Annie enjoys her usual health, my lady, thank you. I must apologise for not having observed Your Ladyship's arrival. Short-handed as we are, I was in the back regions, giving a final touch-up to the silver."

"I see what you mean, Summers: a grievance: no footman. Never mind, I'll come and help you tomorrow: I adore polishing silver; I even like washing up, probably because I never have to do it except for fun. You and I, Summers, will have a good time over the pantry sink. We will tell each other all our secrets—— Oh, Rose, my lovely, my precious, how absolutely *wonderful!* It's you! I don't *believe* it. It seems too good to be true."

She enveloped Rose in a soft, warm, scented embrace.

"And who else should it be but me in my own house?" said Rose. She loved this nonsensical Juliet, her friend and Walter's—Juliet, who had depths unsuspected by those who judged her only by the superficialities of her manner.

"I am so desperately sorry I missed the train," said Juliet.

"There's something about me—I think I must have been born to miss trains. It must have been a curse put upon me at my christening—the bad fairy godmother, you know. We all have one, don't we? And she does different things to all her godchildren; she must have an enormous repertoire in her sense of humour; in my case it was to make me miss trains; well, that's a fairly innocuous thing to do, except that it is inconvenient for one's friends. I *did* telephone, my angel. This is Bobby, by the way; he was an angel; he drove me down; he can't stay to dinner; he has to get back to London; he has to go on guard or parade or something tiresome, don't you, Bobby? I never understand about these things soldiers have to do: I just accept them as a man's job, and all I hope for them is that they shouldn't get massacred in some horrible war. I am devoted to Bobby and I should hate him to get massacred. . . . He is going to help Summers carry my luggage upstairs; is that all right, Rose?"

"How do you do?" said Rose politely to Bobby, this stray young man who had wandered into her house. "Do have a drink, won't you, even if you can't stay to dinner? Juliet, this is my sister Lucy—Mrs. Packington. I don't think you have met before. And this is my brother-in-law, Dick Packington; he is something in the City, I never just know what; and this is my nephew, Robin Packington, who has just come home after four years in the Colonial Service; he is going to tell us all about it, aren't you, Robin? Juliet, a drink?"

"Angel, yes, Gin-and-it, for choice. Unless there are any champagne cocktails? That's what I feel I need to buck me up. I've been so ill. . . ."

"Summers shall make some when he has taken your luggage upstairs. Won't you, Summers?" ("Champagne cocktails!" thought Lucy. "And on Good Friday, too!") "Now come and sit down," Rose continued, doing the hostess, pushing an armchair on casters nearer the fire for Juliet. "A drink, Lucy? . . . No? Just a little orange juice with water? All right, here you are. Dick, a drink? . . . Good! Whisky and soda? . . . Robin? Help yourself. . . . Give Lady Quarles some more; fill up her glass. . . . Juliet, are you warm there by the fire?"

"Lovely and warm, Rose, my sweet. But where's Walter? Where's my pet of a Walter? I idolise that man," she said, addressing herself to the astonished Lucy; "I simply worship him. I'd die for him, if he asked me to, not that he ever would, more's the pity. He just tosses my devotion aside; in fact I don't believe he's aware of it—— Oh, *there* he is!" she exclaimed as Walter and Gilbert came in, followed by Svend. "Walter!" she cried, extending both her hands to him. "My favourite man, Walter, my poppet, how are you? I can't get up. I'm too deep sunk in one of your lovely chairs. Oh, darling, I've been so ill; you don't know. Really feeling like death. I thought I was going to die, but I staggered up out of my bed to come down to you and Rose for Easter. A sort of resurrection, if you see what I mean. Easter is the time for resurrection, after all. I know you don't believe in that sort of thing, but I do assure you that I struggled up out of my bed just because you and Rose were having an Easter party and I was determined to come."

Rose caught an amused glance from Walter: they both

knew, or thought they knew, that Juliet's illness was nothing more than the usual hang-over.

"Oh, *Svend!*" said Juliet. He had come nuzzling up to her, pushing his long nose across her knees. "Oh, *Svend,*" she said, bending down to imprint a kiss on the black patch between his brows. "Your kiss patch," she said. Deliberately he clambered up across her knees, and stood there, very complacent, surveying the rest of the company; his paws dangled, silvery; in proud possession. Juliet stroked him; his ruff was soft as her own furs; his coat was sleek as a top hat. "Oh, Svend, my ducky-diamond, my sonny-boy, my beautiful furry boy, my lamb, my wolf, my savage beast, my gentle one—go away now, you've had enough love to last you for a bit. Go away," she said, pushing him down. "You're too big. You're too heavy. Sit."

"He never forgets you," said Walter, watching.

"Dogs always like Juliet," said the stray Bobby rather resentfully. "She has a way with them, as she has with horses."

"Juliet," said Rose, at last able to get a word in, "I don't think you know my brother-in-law, Walter's brother Gilbert. Dr. Mortibois; Lady Quarles."

"By name, of course," said Juliet, suddenly subdued, looking up almost with veneration towards Gilbert. He bowed gravely in response. "Oh, you *are* like Walter!" she exclaimed, overcome by amusement. "You have just the same old-fashioned manner, rather stiff. . . . Bobby, you had better take a lesson in deportment from them, you rough cub; they'll show you how to behave."

A glance passed between her and Bobby, betraying

clearly what the relationship between them was, albeit a fleeting one.

જ⊷

"Darling Rose!" said Juliet as Rose accompanied her up into her bedroom. "What a heavenly party! Just us, and those nice, cosy relations of yours, and my precious Walter, and that marvellous brother of his, whom I've always pined to meet. They say he does the most extraordinary things with people's brains—puts one in where there wasn't one, and mends the ones that have got damaged. I must get him to tell me exactly how he does it."

"I have no doubt you will," said Rose, laughing. Juliet could always get any man to talk shop to her, however wildly beside the point her own comments might be. Perhaps it flattered them to unfold their views to a silly, lovely woman displaying the deepest absorption: perhaps, also, it was of some value in clarifying their own minds. "You see," Juliet had once remarked to Rose after Walter had spent an hour expounding one of his cases to her, a tricky case, involving several very abstruse legal points, "Walter knows that it doesn't matter what he says to me. It is like thinking aloud. I just say yes every so often, or fancy that! *Fancy that* is a terribly useful phrase: it covers everything, whether you have understood it or not. It fits in everywhere: it's foolproof. Men swallow it like a gulp of wine. It makes them feel that they have been saying something enormously important, which no doubt they have; and above everything else, it gives them a sense of superiority. Besides, I really am interested; no humbug. God forbid, though, that I should ever get entangled with a higher mathematician; that would put rather too much strain upon me as the good listener."

She was now sitting at the dressing table, making grimaces at herself in the mirror as she made up her face.

"Raddled, that's what I am," she remarked to her own image, "but what does it matter? I'm so desperately unhappy, Rose. I've come down here partly in order to consult you and Walter about it."

"Oh dear, have you?" said Rose, who was far too well accustomed to Juliet's desperate unhappinesses to be much perturbed. "What is it this time? Love again?"

"Love!" said Juliet contemptuously. "If it were only love! Though, as a matter of fact, I've got something to tell you about that too; I'll show you his photograph presently. I'm not like you, darling; we all know that you've never looked at any man but Walter. But this is the real thing at last, Rose. No, don't smile; I know I've said that before, but this is quite different. . . . No, it's Micky. He's in trouble, and Walter must help me."

Micky was her son, a scamp, the one stable devotion in Juliet's mutable life.

"Not serious trouble?"

"Very serious indeed. He has been misbehaving himself as usual, and now he's being blackmailed."

"Money?"

"Money—yes, money comes into it."

"Stumer cheques?"

"Worse than that."

"What do you mean, Juliet: 'worse than that'? He hasn't been forging signatures or anything like that, has he?"

"He's done that too, so far as I can make out. He's done

practically everything that he ought not to do. I don't understand these legal things; Walter must advise me; I'll ask him tomorrow. There's worse than all that, Rose, something I must tell only to Walter."

"Nonsense! Tell me!" said Rose. Juliet always preceded her confidences by an assurance that she would never dream of imparting them to anybody else. "Dearest," she would say to her many dearest friends, "there's not a soul in the world I would tell this to, except you; I can trust you to keep it to yourself, can't I?"

For once Juliet met her with a firmness greater than her own.

"No, my rose leaf, not even to you. That's quite enough about myself." She twirled round on the dressing-table stool and was her gay self once more. As ever in this mood —her habitual mood—she gave the double impression of not meaning a word she said, and yet of some inner overflow of sincerity. Rose, who knew her so well, had never quite fathomed her. Discussing her once with Walter, he had said, "Where you are mistaken over Juliet is in assuming her to be a complete extrovert, a most unsafe assumption to make over so effusive a type." Rose had taken this remark away and pondered it: Walter, who never seemed to give any thought to people or their personalities, was so startlingly apt to be right in his rare judgments. She remembered it now, watching her friend, listening with half an ear to her prattle and recalling that recent moment of reticence, so unexpected, so definite, a door shut in her face. Walter himself, when he did not intend to be communicative, could not have withdrawn more conclusively. She was accustomed to it from Walter, but not from the soft, babbling Juliet. Inwardly disquieted, she responded in the tone that Juliet imposed; one must respect the other person's ruling; yet, answering joke with joke and jest with jest, adapting herself to the butterfly dance of their usual chatter, she knew that the claw of tragedy had for one instant torn the veil.

Were people always like this, she wondered, if you saw inside? What would Juliet say if she, Rose, were to expose the secret of her own life? And dear old Lucy, apparently so smug and contented, with her Dick pop-popping away at his pipe; and Dick himself—had he also his grievances and frustrations? And even that boy Robin—as fresh-looking as a three-year-old straight out of his bath—had he also his worries and concealments? She supposed so. Yet there was something about Juliet, with all her levity, that made her more important than any of these small people. Doomed, desperate, the spoilt, the lovely, the born prostitute, she was now in the act of opening out a folding photograph frame and displaying to Rose a series of eight photographs, all of the same man. Rose recognised him at once, a soldier of many exploits, a sportsman, brave, reckless, and a notorious heartbreaker, one of those characters that do occur in real life, not only in novels.

"Tiger Lorimer," she said. "Always true to type, aren't you? But, Juliet . . ."

"I know what you're going to say, so you needn't say it. Look at the photographs instead. Isn't he superb? Tell me, do you like him best in his polo things—just look at his figure, I ask you!—or in uniform—look at all those ribbons, the V.C. is the first one—or in his skiing suit against the snow—I was at St. Moritz with him the other day, he insisted on going down the Cresta, I nearly died of fright—or just in country clothes with a gun?"

"Juliet . . ."

"Yes, I know: heading for disaster as usual. But really, this is different. We're *madly* in love. I've never known anything like it in my life before. . . ."

Rose listened patiently to the familiar recital.

"Wouldn't you like to ask him here tomorrow?" she said when Juliet had apparently made an end. "I could just squeeze him in, I think. . . ."

"Angel, he's having to spend Easter with his old mother—— No, don't look sceptical; he really is. He's going to ring me up."

"From his mother's house?"

"No, from the call box in her village. She isn't on the telephone."

"I see. . . . Look, we ought to get ready for dinner."

"Rose, I do love you, sweetest, dearest Rose."

"I love you too," said Rose, going away with a sigh. She was glad she had refrained from making any comment about that telephone call.

જ⋗

"I did have such a nice talk with Rose," said Lucy to Dick as he, coming up later, was preparing for bed that night.

"Did you, Pudding? I'm so glad. Rose is very friendly, I must say."

"Pudding?"

"What, Poods?"

"You couldn't not call me Pudding, here at Anstey, could you? Just for these few days."

"Why?" said Dick, surprised, halfway out of his shirt, strangled, and muffled. He emerged, with rumpled hair, gazing at his wife.

"I don't know. Just an idea. It doesn't seem to go very well with Anstey. I thought they might think it rather silly, us both calling each other P. Our private joke, isn't it? Rather sacred, if you see what I mean. Perhaps it doesn't matter. Forget that I said anything about it." She got into bed and lay there comfortably. "What did you think of the way they all went on?"

Dick had been stimulated and amused.

"Rather good fun, I thought. And you?"

Lucy also had been amused, but she had her codes, and her voice remained a little prim. Anstey was subversive. Dick must not be allowed to lose his head.

"I thought they were all very cheerful, but they do sometimes say things one usually doesn't mention. And I thought the way Lady Quarles treated Walter and his brother and that young man was perhaps rather familiar."

"Damned attractive woman."

"Oh, very!" Lucy agreed. It would not do to be unconditionally critical; besides, she herself found Juliet Quarles most attractive. "You wouldn't think she had a care in the world, would you? How nice it must be, not to have a care in the world—just to enjoy yourself, day by day," said Lucy, lying back into the deep soft pillows of the Anstey bed. "There's a sort of realness about her, isn't there, in spite of the ridiculous way she talks? As though she had a kind heart, and was a real person under all that silly gush.

And she is certainly very pretty still. And oh, Dick, did you notice the frock she was wearing at dinner?"

"Can't say I did, except that it seemed to be all soft and flowing.".

"Ninon," murmured Lucy, lost in a feminine dream; "rose-red ninon, right down to the floor. French, obviously. A bit low in front, I thought, for the country," said Lucy, who did not know the French phrase *la naissance de la gorge,* and would not have used it had she known it. "Do you think Walter is attracted by her? And what about the young man she called Bobby? Was he a relative, or what?"

"*Or what,* I should say, very definitely," said Dick, going into the bathroom to wash.

"Di-ick," she called out, "have you noticed the bath salts? And the toilet water from Floris?" She waited until he came back. "You really ought to have some new pyjamas," she said, contemplating her husband with dissatisfaction. "I expect Walter wears crepe de Chine."

"Well, if you'd rather sleep with Walter . . ." he said, switching off the light and climbing in beside her.

"*Dick!*" she said, turning warmly towards him. She put her arms round his neck; he responded; and they suddenly acted in a way they had forgotten for many years.

Chapter 3.

RETROSPECT

Daughters of a country rector in Yorkshire, Rose and Lucy had both met their future husbands at a tennis tournament at the local "big house." Considered nice girls, they were often asked over from the Rectory. Dick Packington was then a young man of twenty-five, ordinary, full of animal spirits, and ripe for love. Walter Mortibois, five years older, already regarded as a coming man, had been the target of many a matrimonial shaft, all of which he had gracefully evaded without even appearing to notice them. He had, however, come privately to the decision that he would be well advised to acquire a wife, if only to act as housekeeper and hostess in London and at Anstey; his profession and his ambitions both necessitated a certain amount of entertaining, and although he openly declared, when twitted by his friends, that the comfort of a domestic existence held no allure for him, he now went about inspecting all the eligible young women of his acquaintance rather as a connoisseur might seek, in a leisurely fastidious way, drifting in and out of dealers' galleries, the final piece of tapestry needed to round off the fine taste of his establishment. He was aware that his demands would not be easy to satisfy, but it never occurred to him to wonder if he was justified in making them. He would be perfectly frank. It would be difficult, but he must force himself to it: *take it or leave it,* he would have to say in effect. Not an easy thing to say to a guileless girl to whom you have just proposed marriage; she would have such different ideas probably—romance to start with, babies to follow, and all the rest of the recurrent glamorous story. Even Walter possessed enough knowledge of human nature to know that human nature is not easily set aside: he had learnt that in the law courts. Moreover, he had a definite code of fair behaviour, give and take: he would never, he thought, exact a greater generosity than he was prepared to equalise on his own terms. Kindness and consideration he was ready to give to any extent; patience with a woman's whims—for he preserved a rather touchingly anachronistic view of women, faded as photographs in a family album—but not love, not even domesticity, and certainly not passion. And, above all, no progeny. On that point he was icily determined. *Sine prole* should be his motto. *Après le malheur de naître, je n'en connais pas un plus grand que celui de donner le jour à un homme.* He agreed with Chateaubriand that no greater misfortune could befall a man, after the initial mis-

fortune of having been born, than to pass on the gift of life
to another.

৵

He had arrived at that resolve by a perfectly logical
process of thought extending over all his adult years. He
was no professional cynic, indulging in such keen but
cheap Voltairian quips as might have been expected to
flash from his forensic wit; on the contrary, men were often
surprised to detect in his conversation a certain tenderness,
which, in a less redoubtable man, might have aroused
suspicions of a latent sentimentality. The deep-seated hu-
manitarianism of Walter Mortibois was as proverbial as his
ruthlessness in attack. It was recognised, from phrases he
let slip when carried away in discussion, that a sense of the
suffering and folly of the human race flowed ceaselessly
as a burning accompaniment to the blood in his veins. His
brother Gilbert had once been heard to remark that Walter
was so consumed by love and regret for humanity at large
that he had nothing left to bestow on the morsels of humanity dwelling near him. "When you are always looking
at the horizon," said Gilbert, "you do not observe the blade
of grass at your feet."

It was this attitude of mind, so correctly though incom-
pletely interpreted by Gilbert, that had led Walter to the
implacable decision never, by any act of his own, to assist
in the propagation of his species upon earth. He was pro-
foundly convinced that the human race had better be
allowed to peter out. His mind, his deepest mind, brooded
permanently upon the tragic irrationality with which
Man conducted his affairs. Torn between his admiration

for Man's achievement and his despair over the ensuing, contradictory mismanagement, he could see no redemption ahead. Many philosophers had contemplated in theory the prospect of a dying planet beneath a shrinking sun; Walter was unusual, perhaps unique, in that such a prospect appeared as no theory to him, but as a reality not so impossibly remote in time—time being only relative—and much to be desired.

Meanwhile, one must, he supposed, continue to live. In another age and in another country he might have chosen the contemplative life, but the mould of twentieth-century England and the sheer vigour of his own intellect had ordained otherwise. His pessimism might be too fundamental to allow him the instincts of a reformer, but his natural energy must find expression in work. There was a precision and a logic about the administration of the law which accorded with his temperament and gave him a certain aesthetic pleasure comparable with his favourite relaxation of chess; it was therefore on a legal career that he had decided and at which he was making so apparently effortless a success. Men said he would have done well at anything he chose to take up. Worldly success he regarded with complete scorn, but he did find some satisfaction in a job for its own sake thoroughly done. And, since he had a touch of the hedonist in his nature he would not affect to despise the more elegant pleasures of life; he liked a well-appointed house, he liked good food and good wine, he liked pictures, books, and music, he liked everything about him to be of the best without ostentation, he had no tolerance for the shoddy or the second-rate. It followed, therefore, that in his choice of a wife he would seek to satisfy his taste for the quietly decorative; and also, because of a mischievous twist that enjoyed surprising his acquaintances by an unlooked-for move, he would find her for himself in some obscure corner, unilluminated by the chandeliers of London drawing rooms, and would produce her for all to acknowledge the impeccability of his judgment.

It amused him to think of what he might be taking back in his pocket to London from this week end in Yorkshire.

ॐ

The two sisters were very different, both in appearance and in character. Lucy was fair and fluffy; Rose dark and sleek. Lucy took after her father, the untidiness of whose garments was the despair of his wife; Rose took after her mother, who had a French grandmother and who had transmitted a natural chic and vivacity to her younger daughter. Both girls were given a minute dress allowance, but whereas Lucy bought a number of cheap and amorphous clothes, Rose bought very sparingly and always looked as though she dressed in Paris. Even when Rose, exasperated, insisted on superintending her sister's purchases, Lucy still contrived to look as though she dressed from the village shop. They were very much attached to each other, however, and in many ways their natures dovetailed conveniently: Rose, nervous and irritable, found comfort in Lucy's good humour and placidity, and Lucy, for her part, was satisfied to admire Rose and to say she could never hope to be like her. If ever she felt a tweak of envy, she dismissed it, and was probably the more contented of the two. In her simple way, she managed to have what she described as quite a good time; young men, a little alarmed by Rose, turned more naturally towards Lucy, whereas the older men, amused by Rose's air of sophistica-

tion, set themselves to find out what this improbable product of a country parsonage was really like. Everyone said
from the first that Rose was sure to make a brilliant marriage, taking it for granted that Lucy would marry some
steady, unambitious youth, settle down, and live happily
forever after.

They were not wrong in their conjectures, nor did the
entire neighbourhood fail to be speedily apprised of the
attention Sir Walter Mortibois had shown to Rose at the
tennis tournament. He was rich, they said, somewhat mys-
terious, a baronet, having succeeded his father at an early
age, and the owner of a beautiful place somewhere in the
South of England. Out-of-date copies of Who's Who were
taken down from the shelves for consultation. Poor Dick
Packington, who had been observed to spend most of the
afternoon at Lucy's side, could not be expected to figure in
this publication. Walter, for his part, was not unaware of
the interested glances directed at him, not unaware but
coolly determined. Pleasing to the eye, with a curiously
assured manner in one so young and rural, sufficiently
quick-witted in her conversation, this girl whose name he
did not even know might well be moulded to his require-
ments. Her very air of reserve, which charmed him, he
took as a guarantee that no undesirable emotional complications would trouble their future. Devoid of vanity, it
never occurred to him that he might obtain not only her
hand but her heart.

ૢૡ

Rose had fallen very quickly in love with Walter. She
had been surprised and gratified when he had appeared at

the Rectory on Sunday afternoon, the day after the tennis party, with the suggestion that they might go out together for a walk. They had gone rather awkwardly, for this grave young lawyer was not, in Rose's eyes, at all the sort of person to be taken for a country walk, and the only interpretation she could put on his request was a desire for her company. He seemed unable to negotiate stiles or ditches, and indeed seemed quite unconscious of their surroundings or of where she was leading him. He stumbled on, in the wrong kind of shoes, replying at random to the few remarks she addressed to him. He apparently did not know the difference between a pheasant and a partridge, and indeed did not seem to be paying any attention to what she said or to where they went. Halfway down a woodland ride, however, he took abrupt control, inviting her to pause for a moment and to seat herself beside him on the trunk of a fallen oak. It was here, in surroundings most incongruous to him, that he asked her to marry him.

The conditions he put were hard.

"I will not pretend to be in love with you, whatever that may mean," he said, "but I think we might suit each other, from the little, the very little, that I have seen of you. I have, of course, no means of judging if you can entertain the same thoughts about me. I put forward my proposal in all diffidence, and you must consider yourself entirely at liberty to reject it. I shall not be heartbroken, since my heart is in no way engaged, but I admit that I shall be disappointed."

"Thank you," said Rose. She did not know whether to be outraged or amused; all she knew was that the seriousness of his manner forbade laughter.

"Yes," he pursued as though he were stating a case, "I should certainly be disappointed, for I feel convinced that we might have much to give to one another. I have for some years been considering this question of marriage: I am not an impetuous man, but once I have come to a decision I have no hesitation in going forward. When I met you yesterday I realised that I had reached the end of my quest; I saw no reason for delay; I excused myself to my hostess, borrowed a motorcar without, however, saying where I was going, since I did not wish to compromise or embarrass you in any way, and here I am to present myself. I do not know if you are informed as to my circumstances?"

"I know only what everybody knows—that you are rich, clever, and have a house with a beautiful garden somewhere in the South Country."

She said the South Country because to her Yorkshire mind there was a real difference between the North and South.

"Anstey." It was the first time the name of Anstey had even been mentioned between them. Skipping her references to his being rich and clever, he said, "Yes, I think you would like Anstey. I have also a house in London and spend my time between the two, principally in London because of my work. But I can tell you about all that afterwards. Such explanations would become irrelevant, should you decide not to accept me. For I must warn you that you must accept me only on my terms, which I had better state in advance. It would be unfair to let you commit yourself otherwise."

She had been sitting gazing at the ground, poking little

round holes in the soft woodland earth with the ferrule of her stick, but now for the first time she looked up and subjected him to a long scrutiny. She saw a man with what is commonly accepted as a "legal" face, strong, clean-shaven, somewhat heavy about the jaw, greying hair, and tragic eyes. His hands, she noticed, were remarkably sensitive, long, thin, and beautiful. For all his habitual gravity, his mouth was humorous, and she had already observed that he could twinkle as though with mischief when he was about to make a remark. Today, although his sense of humour had been so ludicrously pushed into abeyance, she found something unusual and attractive about his phraseology, which reminded her of the idiom of some old-fashioned novel; there was something laboriously conscientious about it, as though he were determined to expound his meaning with the utmost clarity in the avoidance of any misunderstanding, painful though it might be thus to reveal himself. She felt drawn towards him as she had never felt drawn to any human being before.

"You are a strange creature, I think," she said. "Go on. State your terms, as you say."

"I want no children," he said simply. "I want my marriage to be a marriage in name alone. You understand what I mean?"

"Yes," she said; "yes, I understand what you mean."

"I will ask you to forgive me if I do not now tell you my reasons for this decision," he continued. "I can at least assure you of two things: that they are in no way discreditable, and that they have no connection with my health or any similar objection; I mean, for example, that I am suffering from no disease or disability, and that there is nothing like, shall we say, insanity or hereditary illness in my family. It is merely that I should prefer not to disclose, at present, what is after all only a personal idiosyncrasy but one which is very deeply associated with my private philosophy of life. Later on, if you become my wife, I may possibly tell you; perhaps never; probably not; I make no promises. There is only one person in the world who has ever received my confidence, and that is my brother. Of course, if you insist, I will try to explain to you, but as a favour I beg you not to. I know it is a great deal to ask."

"I will not insist," she said in a low voice.

"Am I to take that to mean that you will consider my offer?"

"Oh, I don't know!" she said. "This is all so very strange; you really must give me time to think it over. Can I write to you? I don't even know your address! How long will you give me?"

"I have waited so long that I can well afford to wait longer. I have no desire to hurry you. I must go back to London tomorrow, but here is my card with the address." He suddenly put his hand on her knee. "Please decide to marry me, Rose."

She looked at him again, trying to fathom what she could read in his eyes. She could not; there was a gulf of years and experience between them, but the boyish impetuosity of his last remark and his use of her Christian name —the first time she had ever heard it on his lips—did much to diminish the fear she had of him. She began to feel that here was a human being with some appeal to make to her; his nature might conceal some dark secret at which she could not even guess; time would bring it to light. She smiled at him, the first time she had smiled.

"I'll write," she said.

ह�

They sat for a little while talking quietly, making no reference to the conversation which had passed between them. It was warm in the wood, smelling of damp earth; a pigeon cooed, a red squirrel crossed the ride quite near them and ran up a tree. She asked him about Anstey—was he fond of it?—and he told her something about it, how the gardens had been laid out in the eighteenth century by his great-great-grandfather, and how there was a lake where the wild fowl came. He had dropped his stilted speech, talking naturally now; they even laughed, and she noticed what an agreeable voice he had, deep, varied in pitch, with a slight slurring of the letter *r*. (Had she been better informed, more familiar with London, she would have known that that voice, which could be used either as a glaive or an organ stop, was already famous, a powerful asset in his legal armoury.) After a time he said that he must be going back, his hostess would be wondering what had become of him, so they wandered along the ride and came back to the Rectory, on easy terms, good friends.

ह�

Rose said not a word to her mother of what had happened, ignoring the question so plainly written all over her features; Lucy, however, was not so easily to be shaken off. She followed Rose up to the bedroom they shared.

"What on earth have you been doing all the afternoon?

Wasn't it very extraordinary, his coming here like that to carry you off? Now don't be tiresome, Rose; don't put on that shut-up face of yours; tell me all about it. What did you talk about? Is he as clever as people say? Were you frightened of him? I should be! Do you like him? Does he like you? Has he fallen in love with you?"

"No," said Rose; "he hasn't. Do leave me alone, Luce; I'm tired."

Suddenly she discovered that a new element had entered her life: she felt closer to Walter than to her own loved family. Apart from flashes of exasperation, it was the first time she had ever consciously criticised them. Affronted by her mother's inquisitive peering, she now found Lucy's curiosity intolerable, even common. Normally the sisters chattered freely about their small adventures, laughed a good deal over them, made fun, and had no secrets from one another. Her first contact with Walter had taught her different values. The impact of his personality had been such that, even if she never saw him again, she would never wholly depart from his standards. He had provided her with a kind of measuring rod. Strange though he might be, in her eyes even a little sinister, outrageous by conventional standards, he had shown her by implication the value—nay, the beauty, the importance—of dignity and reticence, implanting in her mind the suggestion of whole areas hitherto unsuspected by her, areas in which people cherished what he had called a philosophy of life, so precious and private a possession that they were reluctant to impart their thoughts and, by imparting, cheapen. Had not she herself, instantly responding to his challenge, refrained from insisting upon a revelation? Her whole future might depend upon it; she longed to know; but pride in not failing him, and the respect with which he inspired her, a respect increased by his obvious reliance on her discretion, had made her say, in a whisper of sacrifice, "I will not insist."

She must never insist. Pacing up and down the bleak little bedroom, she worked out her difficulties. Strength was in her nature, but the demand made upon it was sudden and extreme. Too young, she had neither the experience nor the sagacity to meet the demand of this grappling match between the unknown force, which was Walter, and the equally unknown force, though minor, which was herself. With undeveloped muscles and small skill, she found herself locked against an adversary who would win, who was bound to win. Bewildered, she knocked her fists against her temples in a foolish gesture, trying to understand, trying to escape. No sanity was to be recovered that way, so she stopped her pacing and sat on the edge of her bed, pressing her fingers over her eyelids as though she could see more clearly in darkness. (Walter was dark; iron-grey; she thought of him as an iron-dark man.) She tried very hard to think it out. If she married Walter—and by this time she knew, as she had known all along, that she would marry Walter—she would have nothing but her own strength to rely on. He would not help. He would expect her to carry her own burdens. He would not even allow her to help in carrying his. This would be hard; and because Rose was still so young, and still remembered the way he had so very recently put his hand on her knee saying, "Please decide to marry me, Rose," in that voice which had deflected juries, she took her fingers away from her eyes, stared blinking towards the sudden light of the window, and returned to the mood of exaltation.

She might, after all, be able to manage this difficult porcupine. He had said that she must not commit herself. He had said that she could take her time and write. She went downstairs to the telephone and dialled the local number, having first ascertained that her family was safely out of earshot in the garden.

"Could I speak to Sir Walter Mortibois?"

"Miss Rose? . . . What name shall I say, please?"

She hesitated. "Say it is the person he saw on business this afternoon."

"I will find Sir Walter. I think he is playing chess in the library. Is it urgent? Gentlemen who play chess seldom care to be interrupted."

"It is rather urgent. I don't think he will mind being interrupted for once."

"You will excuse me, miss—I mean madam. I mistook your voice for the moment. I quite thought it was Miss Rose from the Rectory speaking. The person he saw on business this afternoon, you said?"

"That is what I said."

"One moment, madam."

ॐ

That was twenty-three years ago, and Rose was now a mature woman of forty-five. Walter was fifty-three. During all those years of marriage they had never had a disagreement; they had lived side by side in a tepid climate of civility, independent, save for a mutual consideration for each other's convenience, but no intimacy had ever come to soften their relationship. Rose supposed that Walter was fond of her; at any rate, she knew that she satisfied him, never irritated him, never bothered him, and understood his external needs. It was something, she told herself rather grimly, to know the daily habits of the man you passionately loved, and what he liked to be given to eat; a privilege of a sort. The only thing that she could do was to serve him, and this she did almost as a religion, not dutiful but transcendental, not in gratitude or as a bargain set against the material benefits he had brought her, but as a passion in itself, a substitute for that other passion she must forever conceal. It was her own form of *mystique*. In the course of years she had acquired a certain tranquility, as though she had ended by muffling the string at the centre of her being, so that it no longer gave out a note, but what this process had cost her was known only to herself. She had been so exaggeratedly careful that even Walter could not suspect. Not by a word or a gesture had she ever betrayed her longing to come into his arms; scarcely by an endearment had she indicated that he was anything more to her than a dear friend. He probably thought her temperamentally frigid, and dismissed the matter from his mind, an accomplishment at which he was an adept. If, sometimes, her physical appearance had prompted an expression of admiration and approval, if, sometimes, he had put out his hand to caress some fur she might be wearing—nothing more than the movement of the natural man towards a pretty woman—he had instantly withdrawn, though whether in alarm as the wing of sensuality brushed past him, or whether on the defensive for the austerity of his principles, she never could determine. She knew him well enough to know that once he had laid down a rule, no temptation on earth would induce him to depart from it. That he appreciated her was evident; a work of art in his house; and she made it part of her service (not an irksome part, it may be said) to render herself as decorative as possible, to give pleasure to his eyes, and to do him honour in the eyes of others. Carrying her years lightly, she was better-looking now than when he had found her in Yorkshire; a finished product of London and Paris, her figure as slight and underdeveloped as a young girl's—she would never lose it, said poor bosomy Lucy—her hair had remained blue-black as the raven's wing, save for one pure white quiff springing back from her brow, startling and unforgettable. She wore her hair brushed sleekly back, gathered into a knot at the nape, and whatever the prevailing fashion might be, she was wise enough never to change it.

Men had admired her, still did admire her; and had she been so minded, she could have indulged herself as freely as Juliet Quarles in one love affair after the other. It had been part of her service to Walter to remain immaculately faithful, "if faithful," she said to herself, "is quite the right word." It had not always been easy; though, sustained by her one fanatical devotion, easier than might be supposed. The world, looking on, could find only the explanation that she and Walter had discovered a rare contentment in one another: some people sneered; others found it, or pretended to find it, touching. Rose suspected that Gilbert knew the truth; she had had two or three rather probing conversations with him, but Gilbert was of far too delicate a humour ever to trespass further than he might

be wanted to advance. She had never found it necessary
to imply even the gentlest rebuke. To less proud a woman,
this unspoken privity with Gilbert might have offered
some touch of comfort, of support; a human weakness, a
relief from the bleak loneliness she had ordained for herself; but Rose lived inwardly on too high a level of single-
devotedness and pride. The most that she would admit,
in her secret thoughts, was that even if Gilbert did know or
guess the truth, his fraternal understanding of Walter
rendered his knowledge endurable, provided he never
spoke of it to her.

One thing she knew for certain: that Walter had divulged
to Gilbert the reason he desired no children. Walter had
told her that much, sitting on the fallen oak in the wood,
meaning that, at some time, he had uncovered his soul to
Gilbert; perhaps once only, perhaps habitually? Gilbert
was therefore the person who knew him best, the deepest
crevasses of him, the ice peaks where the blast of disillusion
blew incessantly. Here was the thing that ate into Rose.
No jealousy of Gilbert: she was only too glad, in her self-
lessness where Walter was concerned, that he should have
this one single outlet. Her physical desire for Walter she
had after years of struggle been able to overcome: it was
stifled, dead. And, anyway, she had often said to herself,
pacing up and down her room at night, twisting her hands,
throwing her head back, heaving her shoulders, breathing
quickly and heavily in an anguish she scarcely understood,
since she was sensually unawakened, anyway, she had said
to herself, trying to regain control, what does the physical
thing matter? (Walter slept just along the passage; she had
only to open her door, slip down the passage and find

herself in his darkened room. "Walter?" she would say. "Walter, my darling?" And in another moment she would be in his bed, and all the barriers would come down.) The physical thing does not matter. The poets have said so.

> *Th' expense of spirit in a waste of shame . . .*
> *Enjoy'd no sooner, but despisèd straight . . .*
> *Before, a joy proposed; behind, a dream.*

Gilbert had given her a copy of the sonnets once as a Christmas present; he had not put a bookmarker into the page, but he had broken the spine of the book in such a way that it always opened at Sonnet CXXIX.

Had he done it on purpose? In her tormented hours, she had often wondered.

> *Before, a joy proposed; behind, a dream.*

She had never known the joy proposed; she had known only the dream, and that had been struck down, withered at the shoot. She knew of these things only theoretically, from what her friends told her, presuming a knowledge she did not possess. She had learnt to pretend: a revelation of her ignorance would have been a betrayal of Walter; her friends would blame him, even make fun of him, and that was a thing which in no circumstances must be allowed to happen. Let people ascribe her childlessness to whatever cause they chose: the secret of her virginity must go with her to the grave.

Chapter 4.

SATURDAY MORNING

"Svend!" said Rose, calling.

She had seen him out of the window, and now opened the hall door, standing at the top of the steps in the pleasant air of the April morning.

He came, worried, in a great hurry, having lost Walter.

"Where is your master, you bad dog? Why aren't you with him? Traitor to your love! Shame yourself; *schäme dich.* Here—go and look for him. Seek Walter! Take the paper," she said, putting the folded *Times* into his mouth; "find Walter. Give it to him."

"Will he?" said Gilbert, interested, as Svend entered the house, conscientiously carrying the paper as he had been told. "Will he deliver his packet? Won't he drop it on the way?"

"Not he," said Rose. "He will find Walter wherever he may be, and he will keep that paper between his jaws until he delivers it. As a matter of fact, I don't think Walter is far off—— Look."

Svend had stopped at the door of Walter's sitting room and was at the door handle, scraping and snuffing. Walter opened it, saw Rose and Gilbert, waved a little greeting; Svend bounded in; the door shut behind them.

"Reunited," said Rose. "Touching, isn't it?"

She turned away, to adjust a branch of flowering cherry in a vase.

"That was an elementary performance," said Gilbert. "It's a poor dog that can't find his own master. But he is certainly most intelligent; I have been observing him. What else will he do? What other tricks, apart from acting as newsboy?"

"If by tricks you mean sitting up begging, or dying for his country, none. He is no poodle. He has his own dignity. Walter would never degrade him, though I have no doubt he would instantly learn anything you tried to teach him. No, it is his wisdom which sometimes surprises me. I am not one of those people who say their dog can do everything but talk; in fact I have never had a dog of my own; if I had, perhaps I might have been tempted to make that absurd claim."

"But Svend is half yours, surely?" said Gilbert, watching her.

"Oh no!" said Rose lightly. "He is wholly Walter's. He treats me with civility because he has natural good manners—you might say he was a born gentleman—but I know that I am only on sufferance. No one but Walter exists in his eyes." She nearly added, "And no one but Svend exists in Walter's," but instead of that she said with controlled moderation, "It is really remarkable, Gilbert, the bond between those two. Has Walter ever told you how he acquired him? I know Walter often tells you things he wouldn't mention to anybody else."

"No," said Gilbert, "I never have been treated to this true-lovers' tale. Tell it to me now. We are alone. Your sister has taken her husband and her son off for an after-breakfast stroll down to the lake. Lady Quarles, your Juliet, has not yet emerged from the mysteries of her toilet. Walter, as we know, is voluntarily incarcerated for the whole morning behind that shut door. We have a free hour to ourselves, Rose; and I might add that you are looking most agreeably pretty in the flowery setting of this familiar room. I retain a certain sentimental recollection of this room in my boyhood, when my mother used to arrange the flowers in it; but my mother was never as pretty as you, Rose, although I daresay Walter and I thought her the queen of loveliness when we were little boys, and, looking back on it, I must admit that she did not dispose her flowers nearly so lavishly as you. The flowers our mother put about seem in my recollection to have been in stingy little bunches, not in these great branches you fling all over the place. But tell me your story."

"Walter went down to Devonshire once—I forget why— fishing or something, I think, and while he was there he had tea in a farmhouse. Curled up in an armchair in the kitchen was an Alsatian puppy, very leggy, with one

ear that pricked and the other that still flopped. Walter
was amused by its self-assurance and the way it had taken
possession of the only armchair, as though the whole place
belonged to it, and after tea he played with it on the grass
outside—he loves all animals, you know. When he left,
the puppy tried to follow him, as puppies will, and when
its owner picked it up it struggled and cried, wanting to
go with Walter. Walter came back to London; I thought
he seemed a bit absent-minded, but I supposed he had
some big case in the offing so paid no attention. A week
later he disappeared, leaving me a note to say he would be
back next day. Well, he arrived home with the oddest
naughty-truant expression on his face, and the puppy in
his arms, reaching up to lick his neck, and all its legs
dangling like a baby giraffe. You can imagine how I
laughed. But he told me quite seriously that he had been
unable to get the creature out of his mind, knowing that he
would never rest until he had gone back to fetch it. He
had fallen in love; they both had. And from that day to
this——" She broke off, and shrugged her shoulders in a
gesture that Gilbert had learned to recognise.

"What happens when Walter is in London and Svend
gets left at Anstey? Doesn't he pine?"

"No, that's the odd thing, he doesn't. I believe he has
such complete confidence that he doesn't even worry when
he sees Walter drive away in the car. He behaves then as
though life were temporarily suspended, gravely polite to
me if I happen to have remained behind, but taking no
notice whatsoever of anybody else. I sometimes think he
believes Walter has left Anstey in his charge, to be handed
over intact again at the week end. The servants tell me he

spends all his time lying at the top of the steps, waiting, except when he goes for a walk by himself round the lake for a little exercise. He will come with me, if I call him, but he won't go with other people."

"Perhaps he thinks that you, like Anstey, have been committed to his care."

"Well, we both belong to Walter, don't we, Anstey and I?" said Rose.

Chapter 5.

SATURDAY EVENING

"Walter!"

"Juliet . . . sorry, you startled me. Yes? Did you want me?"

"I know I ought not to invade your private room; Rose would murder me if she knew. She protects you, doesn't she? A good wife! You were working?"

"I was," he said, putting the cap on his fountain pen; "but now that you are here, do come in. Svend didn't growl when you opened the door; you should take that as a great compliment. Do sit down. Shall I get you a drink? Sorry I haven't got anything in here; I'll ring for Summers——"

"Thank you, I don't want a drink. Not just now. You think I live on cocktails, don't you? Well, perhaps I do, because what else is there for me to live on? I must keep myself going somehow. It's so different for you. You have your work—it keeps you happy, doesn't it?"

"Happy?" he said, reacting in the way that men always reacted to Juliet's interest in them. Although she had done the unforgiveable thing, she was already forgiven. Exacerbated by her interruption, he now found it easy to make the best of it, and ceased to cast so much as a regretful glance at his accumulation of papers. "Happy, am I?" He got up, and walked about the room, thinking it out for himself. "I suppose I am. What is happiness? Expressing the best of oneself according to the best of one's capabilities, whatever they may be? Giving the utmost concentration to the task in hand. *Laborare est orare*—work is prayer —to work is to pray. I prefer work to prayer, myself; and I daresay it pleases God just as well. Happy, you said? It is a shallow notion; no thinking man can be happy; all that we can hope for is to get through life with as much suppression of our misery as possible. We walk down our long tunnel with our little torch lighting inch by inch of our footsteps, and come out into a deeper darkness from the round coin of light, the size of a florin or of the full moon, we thought to discern at the further end."

"Walter, you don't really believe that? What about our immortality?"

"A concept devised by man to protect himself against his natural fear of annihilation. . . . But, my dear Juliet, how have you led me into so unexpected a conversation? I feel sure you didn't come in here to listen to my views on life and death and the life after death."

"To be truthful, I didn't, though I love hearing them. I

came because I wanted to ask your help. Shall we go down to the lake? I feel I could talk to you better out of doors."

"Svend also would prefer it," said Walter; "he likes running after rabbits."

He gathered up his papers and locked them into a drawer after boxing them together like a pack of cards. Juliet watched him.

"How neatly you do things," she said; "you ought to have been a conjuror, a card manipulator. . . . Shall we go?"

ح

It was a perfect April evening. Small feathers of golden clouds drifted across a sky the colour of a thrush's egg. Down by the lake the daffodils were now in their plenty; the only ripple on the water came in rings from a leaping fish; a moor hen croaked, invisible. Walter was grateful to Juliet for making no comment.

"Let us go and sit in the grotto," she said.

They went by the path round the edge of the lake and came to the grotto, a dripping, ferny cave of *rocaille,* inhabited by the statue of a pensive nymph dipping one foot into a great shell of water. She held her few draperies to her breast in a modest gesture.

"I love the nymph," said Juliet, putting her finger tips on to the bare shoulder.

"She is rather like you," said Walter, who had often thought so.

"Me?" Juliet gave a hard little laugh, unlike her usual merry peal which charmed some people and irritated others. "Me? Old? Shop-soiled? I wish I could think so," but Walter was right: there was something nymphlike about Juliet, untarnished despite the life she had led and the many hands through which she had passed. "I like it here," she said as they sat down on the rustic bench provided by the Gothic taste of Walter's great-great-grandfather. "I like it here," she repeated, gazing out over the lake. "Look, Svend likes it too; he doesn't want to run after rabbits; he doesn't want to catch or kill anything; he is lying in one of his beautiful attitudes at your feet: his front paws crossed, silvery paws, waiting, just waiting for you to make a move. How that dog adores you, Walter! You ought to feel flattered by such devotion."

"Yes, he is a nice dog," said Walter, reaching down to put his hand on Svend's broad brow, between his ears. He made the caress carelessly, because he did not want Juliet or anyone else to know how much he loved his dog. Rose suspected it; and that was a thing he could never forgive Rose. She should not have divined his secret love. He had married Rose on a cold unemotional understanding.

"I like it here," said Juliet again; "I like the stillness, and the little drops falling, and the cool damp of the ferns and the moss, and the water stealing away imperceptibly. I wish I could be that nymph and live here forever."

"My dear, you would very soon be pining for Paris and the Ritz."

"I shouldn't, you know, Walter," she said earnestly, "not if I could once break away from everything—from the rotten life I lead. But I suppose it has become too much of a habit; and then I've got too weak a character: I get caught up with things and people that I don't really like or need. I'm not like you, all of a piece. You have your work, as you were saying just now; whereas look at me, what am I good for? If I'd ever been happy, it might have been different; but you know how it was: I was married off to a drunken brute when I was seventeen, and since then, although I've always been looking for happiness, it seems to have been just one damned thing after another." (Tiger Lorimer had not telephoned.) "All my own fault, no doubt," she added; "I never seem to have made a success of anything, not even of Micky."

"Micky?"

"Oh, Walter . . ."

She then told him the long, lamentable story of her son's misdemeanours, ending up by saying on the most pitiable note it was possible to hear in a woman's voice, "You see, Micky is the only thing I've ever really loved. Oh yes, I know I've been in love over and over again, even to the crazy extent of marrying three times, not to mention other episodes. You know all about my official entanglements and I daresay Rose has told you about some of the others. They all counted wildly for me while they lasted—I'm that sort of person, too easily deluded—but the trouble was that they never did last. I suppose I always picked on the wrong person. I suppose I would have liked something permanent, and yet I'm not sure: perhaps I wasn't made for permanence. I don't know. Does one ever know oneself? Except perhaps when one is very old and sits by the fire knitting mufflers and looking back over one's life, when one can just begin to see the pattern that it has made. Or if one is very clever, like you, Walter, clever enough to see clearly all along the way, as one goes. I'm not clever; I have no brains; at any rate, I have enough sense to realise that. . . . Micky was a different thing to me, quite different from anything else; he was the one thread that ran all through the pattern. I saw it clearly ever since he was born. I always see things in colours—do you?—and I see Micky as a bright yellow streak going through all the years of my life. Some patches were red, and some were blue, and others were grey-green, and some were black, dreadfully black, but Micky was always this straight golden line passing across everything. I don't know why; perhaps because he was so fair, a real golden baby. I used to take him to the seaside every summer for a holiday when his nanny was having her holiday; just him and me; I never let any man come with us; I sort of kept myself sacred for Micky, for just that bit of the year. I think those fortnights were the happiest times I ever spent. We used to paddle and make sand castles, and then after I had put him to bed I used to read poetry to myself in the evenings. You probably won't believe me, Walter, but I do like reading poetry; it gives me something I don't get from anything else except music. You would never believe what I got from poetry, sitting on a hard horsehair sofa in a cheap boardinghouse, knowing that Micky was safely asleep upstairs. Horrid little lodginghouses we went to, but I liked that: I did it on purpose; it made more of a contrast with the life I usually lived. Of course I see now that I shouldn't have spoilt him as I did; I could refuse him nothing—I never have been good at saying no. And then I was so miserable most of the time; bouts of mad happiness mixed with despair; truly, Walter, you don't know how often I've been on the edge of killing myself. But there was always Micky, the one thing that was mine and that I thought could never leave me. He was utterly mine, because when I divorced his father he was given to me by the judge entirely; his father was found to be a bit insane, you know, so he wasn't given even the right to see him. Micky was my very own, not only because I had borne him. No one to interfere between us. And then there was his beauty. I don't think I have ever seen a lovelier child, with his long lashes and his curly head—— Oh, Walter, have you ever looked down on the roundness of a child's head, and into the nape of the neck where the hair grows into a little point? The innocence of it! No, I suppose only a woman could see like that. And then as he grew up he became more and more beautiful; a dream of a boy; people used to stop talking, to look up, when he came into the room. That dazzling fairness—— He used to wear butcher-blue shirts, open at the throat. And I, poor fool, doting, more than half in love with him myself, believed him to be quite unself-conscious; it wasn't till I had to take him away from Eton that I woke up to the truth. We had always been so close, he and I, or so I imagined. He was simply furious when I told him that I was going to marry Quarles; he howled with rage; he stamped his foot; he went all hysterical; he said he didn't want anybody coming in between him and me; he said he had always accepted Quarles as a friend coming to dinner, but had never dreamt I meant to marry him—nor had I, by the way: it was only when Quarles made me such a frightful scene and threatened suicide that I agreed to marry him just in order to keep him quiet; he really frightened me into it. I did feel then that Micky and I were very close; but then when he got into that row at Eton I learnt that it is a mistake ever to believe yourself close to any other being."

She bent forward, dipped her hand into the great shell, and passed her wet finger tips lightly across the lips of the nymph.

"To cool you, my cool sister," she said. "Look, Walter, that is the only kiss she will ever have. But I was telling you about Micky, wasn't I? And how I am really the one to blame for the whole thing. If you take on the case for his defence—which you will, won't you?—you must make it quite clear that he was wrongly brought up. You must say that his mother never foresaw what trouble his beauty and his . . . irresponsibility would lead him into. You must say how spoilt he was, and how he always had too much pocket money, so that he never grew up with any idea of the value of money, and that made him not realise when he was going wrong. He was young, he was extravagant, he lived riotously, and his friends sponged on him. He was richer than they were. He was generous, so he gave whenever he was asked. He gave too much. He could have come to me and asked for more money; I would have given it to him gladly; but I think he was ashamed; the reasons for which he wanted it were too disreputable for him to confess to me. What does all this mean, Walter? Is he in any real danger?"

Walter had listened, carefully checking.

"I should have to see him and get a complete statement of all the facts. There may be things he has concealed from you. Frankly, Juliet, from what you have told me I do not think it is a case I could possibly accept. You will understand that one does not readily undertake a defence where there is so little hope of success."

She gave a cry of dismay; her eyes widened; her nostrils dilated; she caught her breath; her hand trembled.

"You can't mean it. . . . You were my only hope."

"I can't work miracles."

"But our friendship, Walter . . . I thought you and Rose were fond of me. . . ."

"My dear Juliet, Rose and I are both devoted to you; you know that. Unfortunately, friendship has nothing to do with these matters; it belongs to a different compartment of life. The most I can promise you is that I will see the boy when I return to London. At present I can see only one possible line of defence, and in order to work out that train of thought I shall have to ask you some intimate questions."

Crushed, she said in a low voice, "I'll answer anything."

Walter took a notebook from his pocket and extracted the pencil. He did so with his usual precise, unfumbling delicacy of touch.

"You said, I think, that when you divorced your then husband, Charles Denham, you were given entire custody of the child. I did not know you in those days, but I have some recollection of the case. You were able, so far as I remember, to prove adultery and cruelty. So far as I remember, the question of your husband's insanity, to which you alluded during our recent conversation, was not raised. At that date, it would naturally not have supplied grounds for divorce, but it might have been adduced as a corroborative proof for the plea of physical or mental ill-treatment."

"No, it was later on that he went off his head for a bit.

Of course I'd known all along that he wasn't quite normal. . . ."

"One moment, please. When he, as you describe it, went off his head, was he ever certified?"

"Oh no, it wasn't bad enough for that. I always believed, myself, that it was only due to drink; he had no head for drink, and it always made him violent. Honestly, Walter, the things I could tell you . . . The bruises he left on me . . . The way he flung me across the room, once, just before Micky was born . . . I could tell you things."

"Yes, I have no doubt you could, but not now. I may have to come to that presently. Charles Denham was your second husband?"

"Yes. The first was Tony Ravenscroft. He was the one I told you I was married off to when I was seventeen——"

"Let us keep to the point, shall we? There were no children of the first marriage?"

"No, thank God," said Juliet, "though I never could think why. He——"

"Please." He was jotting down notes in his notebook. "Micky, or Michael, Denham was thus your first child? The child of the second marriage? Is that right? You have had no other children?"

"Do you really want to know everything, Walter? I'll tell you anything, if only you will help me to save Micky. No, I never had any other children; not *born* children, I mean. Of course there have been times when I had a fright, but then I always took steps about it. It is quite easy, if you know how, and if you can afford to pay. It costs about fifty pounds. I wasn't always very cautious—one gets carried away, you know, and you know what men are; they don't think of the consequences; they don't have to suffer them—but on the whole I've been lucky. Is that the sort of thing you want to know?"

"No, I was referring to children borne, and born in wedlock."

"Oh, what an awful word!" said Juliet, her spirits suddenly reasserting themselves. "Wedlock! It makes me feel as though I had chains round my wrists and ankles, and a great dragging log of wood. Wed-lock! Locked-in! Handcuffs; a shut cell, with a policeman's eye glaring through a peephole. Claustrophobia; no privacy; no escape—I never could endure that, Walter. I like to be free."

"Yes, Juliet, I appreciate your personal feelings, but I would ask you to stick to the point if you want me to go into the case of your son. It is irrelevant to my enquiry, the number of children you have found means to abort. What you were asking me to defend is the case of your extant son, Michael Denham, for whom you appear to entertain a comprehensible if excessive affection. . . . I should like to return briefly to the question of his parentage. This question, you will understand, is entirely between you and me; I should never dream of raising it in court, and indeed it would be most injudicious and improper for me to do so—— No"—he lifted his hand—"do not jump to the conclusion that I am accepting the case. I have already warned you that I am unlikely to do so."

"Yes, Walter," she said humbly.

"Now, as to this Charles Denham, your second husband," he continued; "he is, or was, indubitably the legal father of your child since the child was born in wedlock, however much you may dislike the word. What I want you to tell me, and I can promise you that whatever you may tell me will go no further, is whether you are yourself convinced that this man was in fact the father of that child. The point may prove to be an important one."

Juliet brightened; this was the kind of thing she understood; Walter was coming down to a more human level.

"Well, I really and truly think it *was* Charles," she said. "Of course one can never be quite sure, can one? But I see likenesses to Charles in Micky from time to time—just those funny little expressions, or movements, that give the show away. I often thought how awkward it would be if I suddenly noticed somebody else coming out in Micky; though, I assure you, Walter, I would rather have seen anybody than Charles—I never liked Charles very much; I can't think why I married him, except that he was so mad and insistent. I almost preferred Tony, brute and beast though he was; he was a man, I can say that for him. Charles——"

"You were saying, Juliet, that certain resemblances in your son Michael—tricks of speech and manner—persuade you that he was in fact as well as in law the child of your husband Charles Denham?"

"I see what you are driving at, Walter; I'm not quite the fool you think me: you want to make me say that Micky has inherited his father's insanity. I won't have that!" she said, reaching out to wrench a fern by the roots from the grotto wall. "I won't have it! I won't have Micky called mad, even if it is to save his reputation. I won't, I won't!" she said, tearing the fern, frond by frond, to pieces and scattering them into the shell at the foot of the nymph, so that they floated for an instant and then drifted away. "I won't have my Micky called mad," she said; "he isn't; he's naughty; but he's not mad, and I won't have you saying so."

"Dear Juliet, please calm yourself. It can serve no useful purpose to become agitated at this juncture. What I want from you is facts, not emotion. You can assure me, I take it, from certain resemblances which you have perceived between your son and Charles Denham, that Charles Denham was *de facto* as well as *de jure* the father of that son?"

"I was never taught Latin, Walter," she said miserably.

"I'm sorry," he said; "one falls so readily into one's own phraseology. There are few things more difficult than for the expert to explain in simple terms his meaning to the uninformed ignorant. I should be equally puzzled," he said, turning towards her with his sudden smile that lit his face like a shot of sunbeam hitting a Gothic ruin, "I should be equally puzzled if you suddenly started to talk to me about chiffon or voile and their various merits."

"Oh, Walter!" said Juliet, abruptly switched back to something she understood. "Oh, Walter, what a pet you are! Chiffon and voile—they went out of fashion years ago. Ninon and organdie are what you mean. They sound like *la haute cocotterie* don't they? Doesn't Rose keep you more up to date? Lord, if I was your wife, which I thank goodness I'm not, I couldn't stand your cold ways, or your legal mind, or your general misery; I would have made more effort to humanise you. I adore you, Walter, you know I do; but I simply couldn't put up with you as Rose does. I would as soon live with the Hele-Stone at Stonehenge as with you. I went to Stonehenge once," she said, "on a midsummer morning. I went with somebody I was terribly in love with; it was all meant to be very romantic; but in fact it poured and I had to wear a raincoat, most unbecoming, and then owing to the clouds, the sun never showed himself above the stone, so we were disappointed. Life is always like that, isn't it? The things one most wants to go right go wrong."

"Yes, Juliet," he said patiently, his pencil still poised above his notebook, like a hawk moth ready to dart into the trumpet of a flower; "yes, Juliet. I have no doubt that your observations on life, based on so much experience, are correct. But if I may recall you to what we were saying, you had just agreed that Charles Denham was not merely the putative but the actual father of your son, and were also resenting the idea that your son might be deemed incapable of managing his own affairs."

"I won't have Micky called mad. He isn't. He's just irresponsible and rather wild."

Walter sighed.

"I think perhaps I had better have a preliminary interview with Micky. Could you give me his address? He doesn't live with you in your house, I believe?"

"No, he has rooms of his own. I wanted to keep him with me, but he wouldn't hear of it. If only I could have kept him with me . . ."

"The address please? Or his telephone number?"

He wrote it down in his shapely, scholarly script; snapped the elastic band back into place; restored the pencil, and slid the notebook into the inner breast pocket of his jacket.

"Walter! That horrible little black book lies above your heart. What do you keep written in it? People's lives? People's agonies? Living things? Nothing to you, except another bit of work to be done. And if you bring off another bit of work successfully, it goes to your credit; if you fail, you have the satisfaction of knowing you have done your best: you shrug your shoulders, write it off as a pity, and turn to the next thing on your list. Dismissed . . . Do you never think that if that little book had been made of metal—if it had been a silver cigarette case instead of a book—and if you had been a soldier, it might have saved your life from a stray bullet? Such things have been known to happen. A dented cigarette case . . . Look!" She fumbled in her bag, found what she wanted, and held it out to him, a pocked and battered object. He read the inscription, *H. from J. with love, September 5, 1939,* in a facsimile of Juliet's scrawl, and, somewhat moved, returned it to her without comment. "Don't ask me who H. was," she said, putting it back into her bag; "it saved his life once, as you see, but then he was shot down over London in 1940. He was rather like your nephew Robin; that type; a nice boy, a few years older than Micky. Thank God Micky was too young for that war; he was still at school—— Walter, these things are real. I don't believe, that for all your cleverness, you have ever come anywhere near reality."

"There is no such thing as reality," he said; "we apprehend only through the framework of our five senses. Most misleading. Or if there is such a thing as reality, it is as yet entirely beyond our ken. In our present state of awareness, we have not even begun to approach it. Perhaps some thousands of years hence . . ."

"Isn't Anstey real to you?" said Juliet, looking out over the placid beauty of the lake, a dark mirror. "If not, you must be a very ungrateful man. And Rose? Isn't she real to you? And Svend?"

Svend, hearing his name, got up.

"He's a good dog," Walter said, rumpling the deep ruff the wrong way of the fur. "Lie down now, Svend; don't make yourself a nuisance." Svend lay down at once, his nose on Walter's foot.

"No, but seriously, Walter, you must listen to me. You're missing something in life, you know. You can't live by reasonableness alone. You talk about reality, but there is something beyond what you call reality. Oh, I don't know how to put things," she said in desperation; "I know my life is always in a mess, whereas yours is so beautifully calm and organised, and you could talk me into the wrong and yourself into the right in five minutes. Perhaps if we could be shaken up in a sack together, we might be tumbled out as two better people. That little book of yours, over your heart . . . Do you know that even the cheapest little copy of the Bible has saved men's lives?"

"A cheap little copy of *Les Liaisons Dangereuses* would serve the same purpose," he said, smiling. He was embarrassed and rather bored by the turn that Juliet was forcing on the conversation; he began to think again of the papers he had locked away into the drawer of his desk.

"I don't know what you mean by *Les Liaisons Dangereuses*," said Juliet; "I know only that I am talking to you very very seriously for once. You must not shrivel up like a prune. Hard, and black, and wrinkled, with your heart like the prune stone inside you, rattling about. Walter darling, have you no heart to protect? Have you never suffered? Are you not afraid that someday you may be called upon to suffer? How will you face it when it comes? Will you sit in your loneliness, haunted by the ghosts of all the people you have treated so coldly, stretching out their hands in a circle towards you, asking for your help, too late?"

"Juliet, you should have entered my profession!" he said. "I never suspected you of so much eloquence. No judge, no jury, could resist you."

He was disturbed, nonetheless; and, pulling a fern from its roots, in unconscious imitation of her action, he started tearing it to pieces as he slowly recited the lines:

"Wer nie sein Brod mit Tränen ass,
Und durch die kummerfollen Nächte
Auf seinem Bette weinand sass,
Der kennt euch nicht, ihr Himmlischen Mächte."

Juliet listened, entranced.

"Oh, Walter!" she said. "How lovely it sounds! That voice of yours! My God, I don't wonder Rose fell in love with you! It's not fair to have a voice like that. I don't think I ever heard you speak a line of poetry before. I told you I liked reading poetry, didn't I? But I always had to read it to myself; none of the people I knew were the sort who liked it. It was a thing I had to keep to myself. Look, darling, I'm very uneducated as you know; but I did know German once, and although I got the gist of it, could you speak it once more in a translation? Apart from anything else, I should so love to hear you speaking poetry again, a sort of luxury in our grotto, this evening; a treat to round off the evening, when you've made me so miserable and

I've lectured you in a way I've no right to. Say it again, Walter; say it in English."

"Who never, weeping, ate his bread,
And through the sorrowful dark hours
Sat amid tears upon his bed,
He knows you not, you Heavenly powers."

"God, how true that is," said Juliet. "Oh, God, how poets can pack into four lines what one has always felt. If you had a bit more poetry in your nature, Walter, you'd be a finer man. Say some more poetry to me; say some more; I need it. Say something about the lake; look, how calm it is. Say something about that."

Walter thought for a moment; then he said:

"Über allen Gipfeln
Ist Ruh,
Über allen Wipfeln
Spürest Du
Kaum einen Hauch;
Die Vögelein schweigen in Walde
Warte nur, balde
Ruhst Du auch."

"Translate."

"Over all the hills
Is peace.
Over all the treetops
Scarce a breath.
Little birds are hushed in the forest,
Be patient! Soon
Shalt thou also rest."

"Ah, how I wish I could! Say some more, Walter." She was like a child now, asking for another story.

"It's a mistake to overdo things," he said with a pretence of severity, but really with indulgence, as an adult shows towards a child.

"Do you know," said Juliet, "I believe I was wrong in wishing you had more poetry in your nature; I believe you have a great deal. You hide it, God knows why. Tell me, who are your favourite poets, English?"

"After Shakespeare? Wordsworth; Donne; Hopkins."

Juliet shook her head.

"I like Keats better," she said, "and Tennyson. . . . Your favourite composers?"

He was amused; he smiled down at her with true benevolence, rather as Svend would gaze down, putting his great head between the bannisters of the staircase, on to a favoured guest in the hall below.

"Is this a parlour game you are making me play? If I answer you, will you answer me? I am sure you always play fair. It is a foolish game, of course: how can one possibly have favourites? Very well then: Beethoven; Bach; Mozart; Sibelius. And you?"

"Puccini," she said with no hesitation; "I don't care if you do laugh at me. There is something in Puccini that twangs at me, I can't help it."

"Yes," he said, "Mimi, Butterfly . . . Yes, I see that."

"I do like Mozart too," said Juliet as an afterthought. "Mozart is rather like this grotto, don't you think? Elegant fantasy, half real, half unreal, with the genius to invent it. You know, Walter," she added, "you are not unlike the grotto yourself, with ferns sprouting out of you in all sorts of odd places, and the water springs of your life dribbling away to waste into that vast cold lake. Ugh, it would freeze me to plunge into it. Yes, you are not unlike the grotto, or the lake itself, or the temples beside the lake, chilling and classical. You have something of all those things in you. I wonder if your great-great-grandfather foresaw you when he made this picture for you to inherit. One can't tell, can one? It is the pattern of life working itself out, as I said. Has Rose ever said anything of the sort about you?"

"Rose? No, Juliet, Rose has never tried to interpret me to myself. Perhaps she does not possess your gifts of imagination."

"Now you are laughing at me, Walter; you tease me; there is something of a tease in you, for all your solemnity. It is the grotto part of you, the freakish part; the part of you that I love. The part of you that you don't know in yourself at all. . . . Svend!" she said. "Isn't he a fool, our Walter? He doesn't know himself, does he? We know him better, you and I, than he knows himself."

Svend, aroused from sleep once more, got up obediently, not quite knowing what he was expected to do, but willing to oblige. Puzzled, he sat back on his haunches, looking anxiously up at Walter, waiting for instructions. He cast a look at Juliet, as though aware that she was in some way concerned; but then returned his gaze on to Walter, the gaze of his golden eyes, asking, asking. He slightly moved the tip of his tail; not very much, merely a twitch, to show he was waiting to be told how to obey. He would do whatever was commanded. The pride and the submission of a dog were both expressed in him.

"Lie down, Svend," said Walter crossly. Svend went flat at once. He went so flat that it seemed he could never arise again. He squashed himself down on to the ground, laying his nose flat in a point between his long front paws.

"Walter, what a gift you have for snubbing people! Look at poor Svend! One word from you, and he collapses. Take a lesson from that. If I didn't believe you to be fundamentally kind, I would suspect you of ill-treating that dog in secret. Do you? Are you a sadist in disguise?"

"You may be right, Juliet; perhaps I stick pins into him when no one is looking; perhaps I make him yelp with pain. Perhaps I enjoy doing it. One never knows what people will do when they believe themselves to be safely out of sight. My profession has taught me that. It makes human nature very interesting to observe."

"If you would only observe less, and live more!"

"You reproach me, Juliet; you live emotionally; you are a woman; I am a man. It makes a difference."

"All the same, need you be quite so cold and dispassionate?"

Remorseful, he realized that he had hurt her. He had questioned her as he might have questioned a knavish company promoter, a spiv, uneasily seated opposite to him across the big writing desk in his chambers. That room was designed to intimidate; the ponderous furniture, the sombre Turkey carpet, the black japanned boxes, the desk telephones, the chair which permitted Walter to tilt himself backwards, fitting his finger tips together . . . It was all part of his stock-in-trade. But here he had been sitting in a romantic grotto with a vulnerable woman, a friend of whom he was fond, pouring out to him her anxiety, her apprehension, her alarm, about the thing dearest to her on earth, her son; and he had met her with nothing but his legal jargon, checking her when she strayed from the point, exasperated by her irrelevance, but sufficiently well trained (he hoped) in patience and courtesy to suppress all visible signs of exasperation short of bringing her back time after time to what, in his mind, he called her "statement"; yes, he must blame himself.

He blamed himself the more readily because Juliet's words echoed something he had heard before; oh, the merest whisper, no more than a breath passing his cheek. After-dinner speeches, where he had been the guest of honour, very deferentially and with the lightest possible touch suggesting that for all his brilliance something was lacking—was it the grace of a common humanity? They had never actually said so. He recalled a witticism provoked by his own name, never meant to reach his ears: "Mortibois, Mortibois? Dead wood! Couldn't be better named." He recalled also the words an old judge had used to him in private on the occasion of his taking silk, "We welcome you as our latest recruit, Mortibois; you will go far; but if an old man may give you a word of advice, I would beg you to bear in mind always that a man's temperament comes through, however carefully he may disguise it. A great advocate, like any great man, must have passion within him, the passion which is a belief in his cause. His faith and sympathy are worth more than any rhetoric. Be detached, by all means; in our profession it is necessary to be detached; bridle your passion, ride it as a man rides a fiery horse; but be sure that it is there, for without it no man can accomplish the best that lies within himself."

There had been moments, and this was one of them, when Walter had wondered whether his cold strength was not, in fact, his weakness.

ౘ

They sat in silence unbroken save by the drip of the water; the westering sun laid a blanket of gold over the expanse of the lake. So quiet was it, and both of them so preoccupied with their own thoughts, that a low growl from Svend made them start and look round.

"What's the matter with the dog?" Walter exclaimed. "He must have heard something we didn't hear."

Hackles up, lip drawn back, head swung low, Svend stood on guard. He was trembling; he shivered; he was afraid.

Walter went out, looked up and down the path, looked all round the shores of the lake.

"Nothing," he said, returning. "Why, Juliet, what is it?"

She was trembling too; her lips were parted and her eyes were wide. This was no play-acting; she was in the grip of terror.

"Juliet!" he cried, himself alarmed.

"Don't speak," she said. "Wait. Wait . . ."

His eyes travelled to the dog, and from the dog back again to the woman. They were both as though immobilised, possessed by something which they must endure and which was causing them both some inexplicable anguish. Walter himself was unaware of anything unusual, save the strange behaviour of his two companions; this alone made him uneasy, but some instinct forbade him to interfere with them, as though by so doing he should cause sleep-walkers to fall to their death. Perhaps he knew that even Svend, his own Svend, would pay no attention to him, and shrank from inviting so bitter a betrayal. He remembered those times when Svend, obsessed by the attractions of sex, had disregarded him; when a mere bitch had come between them. He had tried to laugh it off, telling himself that it was only nature, but had been hurt nevertheless, defeated by something stronger than their love, something taking control against their wills, and something, above all, which to Walter was peculiarly repulsive.

Watching Svend and Juliet alternately, he saw a change come over them; the dog ceased to growl, the fur along his spine sank back to its usual sleekness, his muscles relaxed, he looked again at Walter with sane instead of insane eyes. The woman likewise relaxed; she almost crumpled, as though in exhaustion after an exorbitant effort. She passed her hand across her forehead, pushed back her hair, looked at Walter, and smiled. A somewhat wan smile, tired, like an invalid trying to be brave.

"What happened to you both?" he asked, determined to be ordinary and even, if need be, jocular. "Come here, Svend," he added, and Svend came as usual, perfectly normal, to put his nose on Walter's knee and wait for orders.

"I don't know," said Juliet. "It has happened to me before, and I half like it and half dread it. Sometimes it happens for no reason, and sometimes it comes when I've just been through a scene which has upset me, like talking to you about Micky just now, and then your repeating poetry to me. It seemed quite unaccountable, and the only thing

I could fix at all was that it always happened in the country, never in London or any town, though God knows I've gone through scenes enough in towns. I used to think I might be mad without knowing it, but now that Svend has felt it too I feel rather comforted. I shall feel less worried in future. Less lonely. Dear Svend!" she said, putting her hand on his head, his wise wide brow.

Walter, irrationally annoyed that another person should share with Svend an experience from which he was excluded, above all disliked finding himself out of his depth and was resolved to get to the bottom of so odd an occurrence which had assailed, simultaneously, his dog and a lady of fashion whom many unkind and possibly envious people would have described by a different name. All his curiosity and intellectual interest returned to him.

"Tell me more about it," he said.

"Well, Walter, I don't know that I can. It is one of those things that one just *knows* but can't explain. Svend knew it: he was frightened; you saw that for yourself. I wasn't making it up. You see, it is something that seizes one suddenly, like love, or lust, or what I suppose poets call inspiration, or swallows going off to Egypt, or eels to the Caribbean Sea. . . . I don't know," she said helplessly, "I can't explain. It is something quite outside oneself and one's own silly futile life. Once," she said reminiscently and very seriously, "once when this thing came on me, I smelt the smell of goat."

"Goat?"

"Yes. Goat. The smell of a billy goat. Very pungent; unmistakeable. Yet there were no goats about."

Walter was staring at her.

"Are you quite sure?"

"Absolutely! It was a summer night, moonlight, and I was walking in a garden with a friend—not a man, for once. We both stopped dead at the same moment; she had smelt it too. We were both very frightened—well, perhaps not frightened exactly, but disturbed, upset, troubled—I don't know how to put it. It passed quite soon and we walked on. We compared notes and found we had both felt exactly the same."

"Panic fear," said Walter, more to himself than to her.

"What was that you said? Panic? Oh no, I didn't panic; I never do. I didn't panic just now, did I? It is more as though I just stopped living for two minutes; ceased to be myself, and yet became more alive than I had ever been. Do you know what it feels like to go off under gas? The old-fashioned sort which dentists don't use any more, when you felt as though you were swirling round and round in an enormous funnel and were discovering all the secrets of life as you went? And then when you came to, re-entering the funnel from the other end and emerging into a confusion of light with the taste of blood in your mouth, you found you had forgotten everything you meant to remember."

"Very curious," said Walter, "very curious. Most interesting. I wonder what Gilbert would say to all this. This panic fear, I mean."

"He would laugh, I expect. He would say it was pure imagination. Yet I know it isn't. Svend knows it isn't. You saw for yourself."

"The Greeks," said Walter, "didn't dismiss it as pure imagination, nor did the Romans, who were a far less imaginative race. My dear Juliet, there would appear to be more resemblance between you and this nymph in our grotto than I suspected. Tell me, have you ever tried to write down any account of these somewhat unusual experiences?"

"Am I talking now to Sir Walter Mortibois, Q.C., or to darling Walter?"

"To darling Walter, I hope," he said, smiling.

"Well, as a matter of fact, I have. I know you all think me a clown and a silly-billy, but I do sometimes try to write things. Would you, could you bear, to read one or two of them?"

"Have you got them here with you?"

"Well, as a matter of fact, I have. I have always brought them here with me, hoping that I might pluck up courage to ask you to read them, but I have always taken them away again without saying anything."

"Oh, Juliet!" he said, touched by her shyness and embarrassment, and having a sudden vision of Juliet's untidy manuscripts stuffed into her handbag, brought down to show him, and then taken away again. "Who would believe it of you, who are accustomed to sweep in a tumult of petticoats through life?"

"But this is my different life," she said. "I don't suppose I would ever have mentioned it to you if it hadn't been for what happened just now. That tore the curtain. . . . Walter, if I give you some of my things to read, you won't tell anybody, will you? You won't tell Rose? Do you tell Rose everything?"

"There are a great many professional secrets I am obliged to keep from Rose."

"Don't be so pompous; I meant personal secrets."

"I daresay I could keep even a personal secret from Rose, if my confidant asked me to."

"You know how much I love Rose? But somehow there are some things one could more easily tell to a man than to a woman. This is one of them. And besides, there was that funny thing that happened just now, which you saw for yourself. Walter, you are sure that it wouldn't bore you to read my scribblings? They are quite short."

"I shall be honoured, I assure you."

"The famous Mortibois courtesy! Oh, Walter, what an old stick you are! I believe you put on this manner as a sort of self-defence; I've told you so before now. Can you never forget that you aren't in the law courts, and behave as an ordinary man in his home—a very beautiful home, I may say—just look out over the lake in this light, look how the breeze is chopping the water into little coins of gold, like the gold sovereigns our godfathers and grandfathers used to give us on our birthdays when we were young. . . . Wasn't it lovely to be so young as all that—young and innocent? Oh, Walter, how I wish I could recover that innocence, knowing nothing but having only a belief and a faith in life and in people. . . . How tragic it is that one should have to lose it as one grows older."

"An old man once," said Walter, "told me that faith in a cause was worth more than any rhetoric. I have never forgotten those words. The only pity is that I should not have lived up to his precepts. Look, it is getting late. It is nearly seven. We should go back if we are to be in time for dinner. Shall we go?"

"Yes, we must go," said Juliet. "One must always go,

just when one least wants to. The rare moments always come to an end. Walter, you will help my Micky, won't you?"

"Yes," he said with a sigh; "I promise you I will help Micky to the best of my ability."

ટ☙

They left the grotto and walked back round the lake towards the house in order not to be late for dinner.

Chapter 6.

SATURDAY EVENING

"Rose."

He had knocked at her bedroom door.

"Walter? Wait a minute; I'll put something on. I was just changing for dinner. Yes, do come in now. Is anything wrong?"

It was so exceptional for Walter to come to her room that she instantly assumed that something untoward must have happened.

"Walter, what is it?"

He came in; he looked all round, as though he had never seen the room before. He took in all its comfort, all its luxuriance, all the indulgence of a spoilt woman. He looked at the wide bed, which he had never shared. He looked at the drawn curtains shutting out the evening light.

"Walter, don't stand there staring round you like a ghost. What's the matter? Have you lost Svend?"

"No," he said; "Svend is here. But he doesn't know your room, and he is afraid to come in. May he come in? You must invite him."

"Walter, have you gone crazy? Svend, come in at once. There—make yourself at home, good dog, lie down under my dressing table or else jump up on my bed. You're welcome; you're both welcome, but I should very much like to know what brings you here at this hour?"

"Rose . . ."

"Well, what?" she said, continuing to pat rouge on to her cheeks in the lights of the triple mirror. She made the faces at herself that women always make when engaged in this occupation. She was doing it deliberately now because of Walter's presence and because she knew that something had gone amiss with him; she knew him well enough to pretend that nothing was wrong and not to urge him to any confidence. That was the only method by which she could ever get a tittle of revelation from him.

"Well, what?" she said as lightly as she could.

Walter was hovering round her room, touching an ornament here and an ornament there.

"Your clock has stopped," he said suddenly, pausing at the mantelpiece.

"Oh bother, has it?" said Rose. "I suppose I forgot to wind it up." She opened a small drawer in her dressing table, extracted a handkerchief, dabbed some scent on it, put it into her bag, and pushed the drawer back into place.

"There, now, I'm ready," she said. "Shall we go down? Remember we aren't alone; we've got a party."

"Yes, we've got a party," he said. "So we have! . . . Your clock stopped at exactly half-past six."

"What of it?" she said, unable to make out what had come over him.

"I went down to the grotto with Juliet," he said. "I was in the grotto with Juliet and Svend at half-past six."

"Walter!" she said, coming up to him and shaking him gently by the lapels of his coat. "Walter, what is the matter with you? You are not like yourself. Tell me, tell me."

He did exactly what she expected him to do: twisted away from her and resumed his normal manner.

"As you said, my dear, we must go down to dinner. How false a life we lead! Let us, by all means, go down to dinner to entertain our guests. Come, Svend. You, also, will find your bowl of dinner awaiting you. What does it matter to you if it contains horse meat, or rabbit, or even goat?"

Chapter 7.

SUNDAY MORNING

Walter was asleep. The early sun came into his room, half waking him, so that he did not know whether he slept or drowsed or woke. He seemed to be submerged into a half-conscious depth of black velvet contentment, in which all kinds of agreeable thoughts floated round like lazy fish in a warm sea. It was a happy hour. He had had a bad night, as usual; turning on his light at 2 A.M., hearing the clock strike two and three and four, that clock over the stable yard, whose deep note had been so familiar to him since his boyhood. It had a monastic sound, conforming to his chosen celibacy.

It was during those hours of the night that he felt free and almost happy. His secretive nature loved the privacy and the solitude. He took pleasure in reading books calculated to surprise those who knew him only in his other life. Possibly only Gilbert guessed anything of him as he really was.

He returned over and over again to *The Cloud of Unknowing*, to St. Augustine, and to St. John of the Cross.

Svend slept beside his bed, on a palliasse on the floor, in the humility of all dogs lying beside their master. He slept very sound and quiet, except when he twitched and softly yelped in a hunting dream. Walter would then raise himself on his elbow, and look down upon the creature he loved, with the tenderness of a mother looking down at her sleeping child. "What simplicity!" he thought. "The only things he knows are hunger and thirst, pain or well-being, devotion to me, and lust for a bitch." This idea was repellent and caused him to shudder. "Svend!" he would say then, "Svend, wake up. Come up here;" and Svend, disturbed in his innocent sleep, would clamber obediently on to Walter's narrow bed, would settle down with a huge sigh, taking up the best middle part, and forcing Walter on to a knife's edge of discomfort.

Walter was then happy. Holding his book in one hand, he would put out the other hand and vaguely tug at a furry ear. Svend would then roll over on to his back in his most abandoned, vulnerable attitude, all four legs in the air, and the understanding between the sleeping dog and the wakeful man was entirely fulfilled.

It was a little ritual that took place nightly between them.

Towards five o'clock, when Walter's eyes began to droop, he extinguished the light, turned on to his side, and slept. His book had fallen from his hand; his dog slept close against him. Walter was asleep; he did not twitch or yelp in dreams; he was a man at peace and at rest.

Then, later on, the sun came through his curtains, rousing him. He roused himself only a little, just enough to realise that Svend was still there, heavy against him, and that a large bumblebee was buzzing about his room. He lay in somnolent contentment; conscious, but not yet quite aware, and found the furry softness of the dog. "Svend!" he said, jerking at a paw. "Svend, come closer."

Svend crept closer; he laid himself down, stretched out at his full length alongside Walter; they lay there together, utterly happy, utterly confident in one another, watching the bumblebee blunder round the room. They were alive; they had not yet turned into the alabaster of *The Crusader* with his dog couched along his feet.

"Svend," said Walter, "it is Easter morning."

He fiddled gently with the locket on the collar.

"Now why did I say that?" he murmured. "What does Easter mean to me, or to you? Easter Day breaks, Christ rises, mercy every way is infinite—and who can say? So said Browning. Who, indeed, can say? And is it not remarkable, Svend, you indifferent dog, that Shakespeare should have made only one reference to Easter in all his works, and that was to reproach Benvolio, who fell out with his tailor for wearing his new doublet before Easter? A petty quarrel, but perhaps not more petty than most."

He rose from his bed to flick back his curtains on the sunny day, dew sparkling on the grass and rooks cawing in the distant elms. There was already some warmth in the sun, striking on this south side of the house. He could not see the lake from this side, and thought he would dress for a solitary walk before breakfast, when his eyes lit on the untidy pages of Juliet's essays on the dressing table. With a sigh of apprehension, for he feared they would be embarrassingly bad, he picked them up and returned to bed with them. At any rate, they were in typescript; a relief, knowing what Juliet's handwriting was like.

Nothing could have been further from Walter's taste, yet he had to admit with surprise that these ill-composed, ill-spelt, and ungrammatical documents possessed a quality of freshness and originality. The Juliet who had written them was the Juliet who resembled the nymph, with the difference that, whereas the nymph belonged to the pseudo-classic artificiality of the eighteenth century, Juliet spoke with a more authentic voice. Obviously her background of reading was nil; she had not steeped herself in Hesiod or the Greek anthology. What she wrote was myth; but a myth she had evolved for herself, strangely enough not falling into the gaping trap of whimsicality. Her observation was delicate and her pantheism instinctive; without effort she identified herself with the pebbles of her brook, the leaf fallen on her path; Walter expected to hear the dry rustle of a lizard flicking across the paper. He put the pages down and lay thinking of Juliet as she appeared to the world. "Very odd," he murmured. A line of verse came into his head:

Her natural, Greek, and silver feet.

"Come, Svend," he said; "let us go and say good morning to the nymph and tell her what a fraud she is. But first come and let me put on the red ribbon I had prepared for you, to make you smart for Easter. Red, the colour of the flower of Adonis. The flower of Resurrection." He tied the ribbon deftly into a bow on the dog's collar; the fur was soft to his touch. Svend patiently endured this decoration, supposing it to be one of the things he must suffer at his master's whim. His master seemed pleased: he lay back on his pillows, admiring the effect of the red bow; he laughed at Svend, seeing him thus decked out; Svend did not like being laughed at but accepted the laughter of his god as he accepted every dispensation his god was pleased to bestow.

Walter got up; he pulled on a shirt and a pair of grey flannel trousers; he felt young; he let himself out of his house with his dog; he was happy. Svend was happy too. This was a treat, to be taken out so early, before breakfast, alone with his master. He galloped about, bringing his little bits of sticks to drop at Walter's feet. Walter threw them for him to retrieve. They were like schoolboys playing a game. They went down to the lake, and Svend plunged in, scaring the moor hens, and Walter laughed at him as he emerged, dripping, shaking himself dry all over Walter's trousers, as dogs will do even although they have plenty of room to shake themselves dry elsewhere. They were irrationally happy. They did not go near the nymph's grotto. They stayed out in the open, playing on the edges of the lake. Everything seemed very fresh and young and clean.

"Come here," said Walter, sitting down on a bench. Svend came at once, close beside him. They sat quietly. "It is Easter morning, Svend," said Walter; "Easter morning.

But we cannot have it to ourselves, we have to entertain an Easter party."

Then he saw that his fingers were tinged with pink. He looked down at Svend in alarm: could the dog have got injured? His throat and chest were red, as with new blood. For one moment Walter felt a helpless fear; he wished Gilbert were with him, Gilbert the experienced surgeon, to stanch the bleeding. Then he saw the cause, and laughed again, laughed at poor Svend, who could not understand the reason for his laughter but knew only that he was being made a mock of.

"Svend," said Walter, "I thought you were dripping blood, but now I see that it is only the dye off your ribbon that has run. It just shows one, doesn't it, that one should never dramatise events. Events seldom turn out to be as dramatic as they should, poetically, be. One mistakes a cheap dye for the heart's blood. I must clean you," he said, pulling up some tufts of grass to wipe the red off the fur. "I can't have you going home looking as though someone had tried to murder you."

Chapter 8.

SUNDAY MORNING

"Dick, Rose hasn't said anything about church yet and it is nearly ten o'clock. Of course we would have liked to go to early service, but nobody suggested it, so I hoped for the later service at least."

"Did you ask her?"

"I didn't like to," said Lucy; "I thought if I came down to breakfast carrying my prayer book with my handbag—my new handbag, the one you gave me this morning, you generous extravagant Dick—it might remind her. But it didn't."

"We had pink boiled eggs for breakfast," said Robin, "but they were very like ordinary boiled eggs once you got inside."

"Boiled with cochineal," thought Lucy. She knew that trick of old; when Robin was a little boy she had always boiled his eggs for his Easter breakfast in cochineal; it hurt her to find that he had forgotten.

"Do you remember, Mummy," said Robin, "you always produced a pink egg for my breakfast on Easter Day? I used to wonder how you did it. I thought you must have laid it yourself. It seemed miraculous to me; it still does; and when I found a pink egg for breakfast this morning I felt like a little boy again."

Lucy expanded all over; she beamed; she was a happy woman. Dick's next remark deflated her:

"Perhaps pink eggs is all the notice they take of Easter here."

Lucy, remembering the Rectory in Yorkshire, looked pained. She was not feeling happy about her sister, for in her slow but persistent way she had reached the conclusion that a vacuum existed beneath the glitter and luxury of Anstey. People, in Lucy's opinion—and who shall gainsay her?—could not live satisfactorily without love and faith, and although Rose and Walter were manifestly the best of friends, their relationship could not in any way be compared to the close, simple understanding that prevailed between Dick and herself. These two days at Anstey had already done much to confirm a suspicion which she for years had endeavoured to reject. In London she saw very little of Rose, and never except by chance saw her and Walter together. Did she, Lucy, bore Walter? she wondered. Did Rose, in London, keep them deliberately apart? Did Dick—was it possible?—also bore Walter? The thought hurt her: how could she entertain such an idea about her

Dick! But the Anstey influence worked potently, and, although she wanted to cover her eyes and run protesting away, she was no longer quite so blind. Many dykes may begin to leak between a Friday evening and a Sunday morning, especially if the weevil of suspicion has been, beforehand, preparing his little tunnels in the dark.

ॐ

"We shall have to walk to church," said Dick.

"Six miles there and back, and be late for luncheon?" said Robin.

"Robin, you wouldn't think of *not* going?"

It was on the tip of Robin's tongue to say that he certainly would, but as he retained a remote affection for his mother he desisted.

"Well, if we are going to walk we must start now," said Lucy with sudden determination; men were so passive; they needed a woman to mobilise them.

"Robin, you've got your prayer book, haven't you?"

"Oh, Mummy! No, I haven't. I forgot to pack it."

"We gave it to you, do you remember, for your sixth birthday? Daddy and I gave it to you as a joint present, nicely bound in leather. It cost us quite a lot of money— two pounds, I think. Why haven't you got it with you now? You haven't lost it, I hope? Left it behind in Africa? Well, boys will be boys, I suppose, and you can't put old heads on young shoulders. Still, all the same, Robin, I do think you might have remembered to pack it. It wouldn't have taken up much room, and anyway, I should have thought it was a thing you always wanted to have with you. One's prayer book! How can one do without it? Especially as Daddy and I gave it to you . . ."

Fortunately for Robin, his aunt Rose, in whom he guessed an ally, came in at that moment in a flowered frock, carrying daffodils.

"Such a spring morning!" she said. "And Juliet hasn't even got up yet. Johnson will bring the car round at twenty to eleven to take you good people to church. Johnson joins the congregation, I believe, so you need not feel you are keeping him waiting. If you want to stay on after the service you must tell him. For all I know, he may want to stay on after the service too."

In a timid missionary spirit Lucy murmured, "Aren't you coming, Rosie?"

"Me? The vicar would be surprised. I once went to a village wedding five years ago."

"Oh, Rosie, what would Daddy say to hear you speak like that?"

"Daddy is where he can't hear, luckily for him."

Lucy could not help saying, "Are you so sure?"

Rose gave her a glance and half-smile; did not answer; and turned to her nephew.

"Are you going, Robin?"

There was a wavering moment; Rose's manner, which had been uncomfortably defiant, was now mischievous, experimental. She had a mild liking for Robin, but, not having paid much heed to him, had not yet decided what he was like. She had noticed only that he listened with attention to an argument between Walter and Gilbert on the Mendelian principles of heredity after dinner the night before.

She now observed with amusement the struggle she had provoked. Robin looked at his mother, and then at his father, who had wisely disappeared behind the extended sheets of the *Sunday Times*.

"It's Easter Day, Aunt Rose."

ॐ

Rose saw them off, waving to them from the top of the steps as the car took them away. She was in a confused state of mind. Lucy's presence at Anstey on Easter Day had had the effect of carrying her back to the Rectory, their home. She could smell again the peculiar spicy smell of hot cross buns at breakfast on Good Friday. She could see again the sheaves of white lilies and almond blossoms which she and Lucy had helped to arrange in the church. She heard the tinkle of coins falling into the offertory plate. She heard the pure solo of little Denis Larkin, who was so naughty that only his voice kept him in the choir. How homely it had all been, how untroubled! Yet even in those days she had often been irritable; cross with Lucy for her untidiness, snappy to her mother; and vaguely aware that the place cramped her, though she never got so far as deciding that her destiny should lie beyond. The chance arrival of Walter had determined that, and the emotional effort of the succeeding years had never allowed her to stagnate. It had been escape in a way; she supposed that she did not wish herself back; she supposed that the prolonged effort had been worth while.

She sat down on the top step, enjoying the warm sun, pleased that for a few moments she could be alone, without interruption from friends, relations, or servants. She had been feeling hemmed in; she wanted a quiet moment of Easter to herself. Soon Juliet would appear, in the usual turmoil; and probably before that, Gilbert. She would have to pull herself together to talk to either, separately, or to both; meanwhile, this was a very welcome snatch of peace.

Not of long duration, for here was old Summers coming out with a cushion.

"The stone is too cold for you to sit on, my lady," he said reproachfully, putting it down for her in his nanny way.

How kind of Summers, how thoughtful. She moved on to the cushion, wishing that she need not always be watched and tended. But it was certainly more comfortable. She was really fond of the old man, and often felt that she ought to display a greater interest in one who served them so humbly and so well.

"I see you've been cleaning shoes, Summers," she said with a smile.

Everybody knew the story of Summers' implement for cleaning shoes. It was his most treasured possession, and the polish it enabled him to produce on shoe leather was his pride. He had it now in his hand, and looked down at it lovingly, rubbing a finger along its surface.

"If Your Ladyship would care to handle it . . ."

It was a bone, but no ordinary bone: its virtue lay in its being the shinbone of a stag. No other kind of bone would do. It had been bequeathed to Summers as a very young footman by a very old butler who in turn had used it all his life, so that Rose and Walter had once worked out its term of service at over a hundred years. Thanks to all these circumstances, starting with the noble beast roaming over his native moors, it had become invested with a sort of magic: Mr. Summers' bone was an object of superstition in the household. Apart from this occult glamour, it had grown into a thing of beauty, of the purest, most essential kind; innocent of all ornament, it depended upon nothing but the rightness of its own function.

Rose, who had often been allowed to hold it, knew what she was expected to say.

"It's like ivory, Summers, isn't it?"

"I never did anything to it, my lady; nothing but polish, polish, polish."

The car had disappeared round the bend, her thoughts following it like a flight of those restless birds which can never alight on the waters of the Bosporus. Should she have gone, merely to please Lucy, even though her conscience stopped her with a dread of blasphemy? She could not take part in a ritual she no longer credited. Walter's relentless honesty had soaked its stain into her character. Yet, because she was fond of Lucy and wanted to make this Easter happy for her, especially in her reunion with Robin, she wondered whether for once a little kindhearted humbug would not have been more acceptable to God: she could have explained her motives privately to Him. But then, if she felt the implication of blasphemy and also the necessity for explanation, it must mean that she still believed in the Divinity she had rejected. Her confusion increased. She prayed nightly for Walter's safety, since fear of disaster haunted her all the time. Were her prayers, then, only a form of superstition, a kind of "touchwood," just in case, just to be on the safe side? To whom was she really addressing them? And even if she were addressing them to "God," what effect could she expect them to have on that incomprehensible Being? Either He had already made up His mind what calamity He held in reserve (or, alternately, what safety and smile of fortune), or else He had not. If He had, it seemed unlikely that her petitions could deflect Him from His purpose; if not, it seemed equally improbable that He would lend a listening ear to her suggestions and decide accordingly.

It was a long time since she had asked herself these questions; she supposed, rightly, that Easter Day had brought them back into her head. Did Juliet, she wondered, ever worry like this during the short intervals between lover and lover? Poor Juliet, she had something on her mind; something to do with Micky, her son; something she would tell only to Walter. Rose hoped that Walter had not shown himself too stern. He had certainly been in a very strange mood when he came into her room before dinner last night, saying amongst other things that he had been down to the grotto with Juliet. Presumably she had taken, or more likely made, that opportunity to consult him about Micky's troubles, but even so she could not imagine Walter being so much upset by the mere story of a boy in a scrape. He heard far too many of them, and in any case knew Juliet well enough to attribute half her recital to her habitual exaggeration. Something much more important must have happened, something which had given him a jolt. Was it possible that Juliet, carried away by intimate confidences and the suggestive mood of an April evening, had shocked him by attempting too close an approach? She thought that over. It was unlikely but not out of the question where flirtation was so much of a second nature. Juliet would mean no harm; she might even think it salutary for Walter to be prised up for once from what she called his Gothic-effigy sepulchre; and in any

case she would come laughing to Rose in complete can-
dour. "Would you believe it, darling, I made advances to
Walter and he *actually responded;* wasn't it good of him?"
Or, alternately, "Darling, listen, I made advances to
Walter and he utterly turned me down. I'm not used to
being turned down. It is usually me that does the turning.
So good for me for a change, don't you agree?"

Rose, still sitting on Summers' cushion, smiled at the
very idea. She wondered idly whether, in the unthinkable
event of Walter responding to the blandishments of another woman, she would feel any pang of jealousy. She
thought not; after all these years of refrigeration her feelings had become only too effectively frozen. Tenderness
remained, and an unutterable love, but nothing so warm
and natural as physical jealousy. Still, one never knew.
The incalculable heart could wake up to play strange
tricks. She tried hard to imagine Juliet in Walter's arms in
the dark, Walter's hand seeking Juliet's breast, Walter's
voice murmuring words of passion and desire—— No, she
could not imagine it. No spark was struck.

Her thoughts reverted to Lucy, Dick, and Robin. They
must be in the church by now; they would have knelt
down in a row of three, father, mother, and son, on those
stubborn hassocks of red rep, for a moment of silent prayer,
their elbows propped on the pitch-pine shelf, their faces
sunk into their hands—Lucy's hands gloved, Dick's and
Robin's bare—then they would have hoisted themselves
backwards, decently, to sit on the pew in the same row of
three, waiting for the service to begin. Lucy and Dick had
their own prayer books with them; Robin had not. Robin
would have picked up one of the prayer books provided by

the church, also a copy of *Hymns Ancient and Modern*, bound in that peculiarly mournful wrinkled black leather esteemed suitable for the worship of the Creator of all beauty. Robin, her nephew. What sort of young man was he? Rose did not know. Perhaps he had his troubles too, even as Juliet had her troubles, and Lucy and Dick might have their troubles, and Summers with his torn loyalties between his devotion to Walter and his Communistic beliefs, and Rose herself with her strangled love for Walter?

"Poor us!" she thought. "Poor all of us!" And that seemed to be the summing up of her Easter party.

She sat on, warming herself in the sun, in the peace of Anstey—Walter's Anstey. Walter himself was buried deep in his own room, working. Svend would be there too, Walter's dog, admitted to Walter's privacy. He did not impinge in any way on Walter's privacy; on the contrary, he enhanced it; a silent presence, loving, patient, dedicated. Rose could not be jealous of Juliet, but she could be envious of Svend. Jealousy and envy were two very different things.

She heard footsteps within the house, footsteps muted every now and again as Svend's nails were muted when he crossed the rugs, and got up reluctantly to go indoors to take up her duties as a hostess. Was it Juliet? Was it Gilbert? It was Gilbert. She greeted him gaily. Then, because her mind was still dwelling on her own family sitting in church, she said:

"That nephew of mine should be in the Diplomatic, not the Colonial, Service. He got himself out of an awkward situation with great skill just now; he contrived to please his mother and yet to convey to me that he and I had a secret understanding."

"In short, you had been teasing him? Charming woman though you undoubtedly are, Rose, I do not think that you have a very nice character."

Rose laughed; Gilbert was privileged; he could say what he liked.

"I sometimes think that you are like the jester in a play," she said; "one of us, but not really with us; observing us all, and seeing far more than is given to us to see. A kind of melancholy Jacques. No, I have not nearly so nice a character as my sister, and yet she hasn't had nearly so easy a life."

"Trials are said to be beneficial to the soul."

"Then I had better cultivate a few trials," said Rose lightly. "You see, I have things too much my own way. A brilliant husband, a lovely home, heaps of money, pretty clothes, plenty of friends, a brother-in-law of whom I am curiously fond—what more could any woman ask for?"

"Love," said Gilbert surprisingly.

"Love? But, my dear Gilbert, what about Walter? Faithful to me, devoted to me in his way—you must remember that he is a very busy man—never looks at any other woman . . ."

"Not even at you, save as an ornament," thought Gilbert, surveying the pretty picture that Rose made in her flowered frock, balancing herself on the arm of a chair, the blue smoke of her cigarette curling round her head. "A veil of disguise," thought Gilbert; "the modern yashmak; all too transparent. Wreathed in it, she believes herself safe in uttering her pitiably conventional phrases."

"You smoke too much," he said.

"Yes, Dr. Mortibois, I don't need Harley Street to tell me that. A bad habit, no more."

"A nervous trick. You should break yourself of it."

"Dear Gilbert, I don't possess the strength of character. Apart from having a nasty character, as you pointed out just now, I have also a weak one. Shall I tell you something? I live in fear. Is that a cowardly thing to say? Not a day, not an hour passes without my imagining some disastrous happening. And what frightens me most is the knowledge that I should have no reserve of strength to meet it. I live in terror lest some demand of courage should be made on me, with which I could not cope. I feel like a person who at any moment might be called upon to lift an enormous weight, knowing full well that he had no muscles, no biceps. An athlete gone soft, out of training."

"Can you ever have been an athlete, Rose?" he said with unusual tenderness. Despite her elegance and sophistication, he saw her as something soft and small, unarmoured, incompetent, struggling, and vulnerable. "An athlete of the spirit," he added, lest she should misunderstand.

"Gilbert, I like talking to you. I seldom do. We meet in London, and then Walter is there, and other people; we are not alone; and I am just the hostess, and you are one of the guests at our table. It is different down here at Anstey. We have more time, more leisure; we can spend the morning sitting in the hall, talking ourselves out to our hearts' content. My family has gone off to church. Walter is, as usual, working. The only thing likely to interrupt us is Juliet, who will descend presently from her bedroom in a flurry of agitation because she has not received a telephone call she expected."

"Never mind about Juliet," said Gilbert. "Tell me more about yourself. Tell me about this fear you live in."

"Am I talking to Dr. Mortibois or to dear Gilbert?"

"To dear Gilbert, I hope. We are not in my consulting room. We are brother-in-law and sister-in-law; a pleasant relationship, I think, entailing no obligations except those which a mutual affection may suggest. A very convenient relationship. Supposing you happened to dislike me, or I happened to dislike you, we need never meet except on family occasions, funerals, and so on, or when you and Walter felt it incumbent on you to ask me to dine with you in London once every six months. As it is, we can sit here placidly and happily, talking together; no one, not even Summers, will suspect us of an illicit intrigue; we have a background of common knowledge; we share, in a sense, Walter and Anstey—you must remember, Rose, Anstey was my home as well as Walter's when we were boys; I know it inside out, even as he does. I know every leap of the fish in the lake and every drip of the water in the nymph's grotto; only I made the mistake of being born the younger son."

She was grateful to him for talking on at random, giving her a chance to consider what she intended to say. Not that she had started out with the intention of saying anything.

"You are an extraordinarily understanding person," she said. "I suppose it is your job in life. Do you want to worm secrets out of me? I have none of any interest; you will be disappointed. Though I suppose we all have something, even my simple Lucy, which we scarcely admit even to ourselves."

"You were talking about fear," he reminded her.

"Fear . . . Yes, it is a horrible companion. People say, don't they, that it springs from a hidden feeling of guilt? But I am not aware of any guilt. I don't think I have committed any major wrong; I have been self-indulgent, certainly, which leads to a degree of selfishness in so far that one is living for oneself, but I have not lived for myself entirely. . . ." She stopped; she would not mention Walter's name. "The truth is," she continued, "that I am a thoroughly useless person—a parasite. And, as I have just told you, a coward into the bargain. I find the contemplation of life unbearably terrifying. This dreadful sense, which never leaves me, of the calamities which may be waiting to leap out at us. The unfolding future . . . Mind you," she said, "my forebodings are not wholly on my own account; I must do myself that justice. It is not so much that I imagine myself attacked by some hideous disease, or stricken with blindness, or smashed to pieces in an accident, as that I imagine such things happening to anyone I love."

"To Walter?"

"Of course to Walter. But there are other things," she rushed on, evading Walter. "The thoughts of war, and the ugliness of hatred between men, and the impossibility of foreseeing any outcome, any solution bringing understanding and tolerance and peace. You must think all this absurdly trite," she added, "and so it is, but the only thing that can redeem it from its triteness is the absolute reality it means to me. Scorching, searing . . . I do not exaggerate."

"I am sure you do not. The early hours of the morning are the worst, I find. When you lie awake between two and four o'clock."

"So you do understand, Gilbert? Is it possible?"

She looked so much surprised, and so much relieved, that he felt almost mean at having played this obvious little trick on her.

"My dear," he said gently, "do not imagine that you are alone in your anxieties. If you were to delve into the hearts of half your friends, you would find a parallel. I don't say that it would always take the same form: the variations of human nature are as manifold as the variations of human faces, which God knows are astonishing enough, considering that He had only two eyes, a nose, and a mouth to play with. I don't know, either, that it brings much comfort to be told that others endure much the same apprehensions as you yourself endure, any more than a personal tragedy is alleviated by the knowledge that something far worse has happened to somebody else. We are all egoists at heart; or, to put it less unkindly, our own sorrows are just about as much as we have the strength to take on."

"You have an immense pity, Gilbert."

"More than Walter, should you say?"

She shied away from the mention of Walter; he could not coax her yet.

"Why do I talk to you like this?" she said. "I never have. I never talk to anybody. My friends talk to me, but not I to them. In fact I dislike the readiness with which most women will tell you their most private thoughts, even the details of their private lives. Such confidences cease to have any value at all; they go too cheap, six for a penny."

Gilbert looked at her. He knew he must be wary in his advance; the bird would be easily scared.

"You describe yourself as weak," he said, "yet you have a strength of reserve in you which reveals anything but weakness. Shall we say we are talking like this because there is something propitious in the air today? A queer influence working on us from afar? Reaching out over two thousand years? After all, it is Easter morning."

"And what does it mean to you, Gilbert? I thought you were like Walter, unaffected by the Church or the feasts of the Church."

"And like yourself, also?"

"Yes, like myself *now*. Once it meant so much to me, or I was taught to think it did. As you know, Lucy and I were the daughters of a parson, brought up in complete acceptance. Lucy has kept her acceptance, I haven't. I am not saying that Walter ever tried to destroy my faith, such as it was; he would never do that. There is no wickedness in him. But just living with him, day after day, year after year . . . A sort of intangible pressure; a silence; a void. I daresay my beliefs were never very strong; they were imposed upon me in my home, possibly not so natural to me as they were to Lucy; and so perhaps I was a good subject for Walter's agnosticism to work on. Even though he never expressed it openly; he doesn't talk about such things. Perhaps they don't interest him; I don't know. At any rate, he and I have never talked about them; only, sometimes, when I have heard him getting into a discussion with his friends, after dinner as it might be, and just sat listening, I have realised his attitude. It wore me down very gradually; it took a long time—about five years. It wasn't a very painful process, because I had no wish to put up much resistance. I struggled a bit at first. But now you see me as Walter's completed accomplishment."

She paused, blew a smoke ring, and then said, "Do tell me what Easter means to you."

"I suppose that, like Walter, I am a pagan; certainly an agnostic; Christianity has never touched me, save as an exquisite legend, a vision of what might be, a strange poetic tale, man's invention to supply his need. His very urgent need. For the foundation of man's life is fear, believe me or not. Oh, perhaps not the personal forms of fear which worry *you*, Rose, but a far deeper fear, the fear of the inexplicable, the unknown, to which we have decided to give the name God. *Si Dieu n'existait pas, il faudrait l'inventer* —a profound though hackneyed remark. I commend it to your consideration. If God did not exist, we should indeed have been obliged to invent Him. Shakespeare should have immortalised that thought, but by some extraordinary lapse in his universality Shakespeare never made generalisations about God. That is by the way; it is a *marotte* of mine with which I will not trouble you. It is an interesting point, which Walter and I have often discussed together. Perhaps someday, when I have time, I will write a dazzling essay on Shakespeare's disregard of God, and I will dedicate it to you, Rose, in memory of this Easter morning."

"Gilbert, don't fly off at a tangent; you are as bad as Walter. He always evades the issue. Go on telling me about the fear of the unknown and the inexplicable, and about Christianity and the lovely figure of Christ, and what you yourself feel about Easter and the Resurrection. Do please tell me."

"Shall I take your points in order, as Walter, my brother, would do in a legal case? The unknown and inexplicable must at all costs be explained, or at any rate personified and then placated; hence the conception of God, common to the savage in the jungle as to the civilised man catching his bus in London at the rush hour. Hence, having arrived at this appalling conception of an outside force, too heavy for the ordinary soul to carry, we go a step further and transform God into a loving God—*le Dieu* must become *le bon Dieu*, the loving Father, taking care of us all, and each one of us personally. Our own experience denies this; but still we obstinately believe. Fear must be replaced by reassurance and comfort. We are weak; we are afraid; we bolster ourselves up with beliefs which, if we examined them closely, we should soon start to question. And then—it is a logical sequence, having invested the Deity with the attributes of loving kindness and mercy, but still finding Him too aweful in His majesty, we look round for a bridge of approach, an intermediary, a connecting link between the human and the divine: we evolve the inevitable figure of Christ. I put it in the most elementary way, but that is the gist of my interpretation. The humanity of Christ softens our dread; we are not strong enough to do without Him."

"You are a rationalist, Gilbert, and you make it all sound plausible enough, but how do you explain certain experiences which I can only call the experiences of revelation? Surely these are beyond our comprehension? Surely they indicate the existence of a reality somewhere? They act like doors opening from time to time in the darkness, just enough to let the favoured person see the light within."

"There are those who would tell you that all such experiences proceeded from the imagination," he said, "but I am open-minded enough to pass no judgment. I cannot tell. The revelations vouchsafed to the great mystics, and even, in lesser degree, to more ordinary people, are indeed a stumbling block in the path of those who, like myself, would explain the whole structure of Christian belief in terms of reasonable probability. As a man of science, I should perhaps not admit this, but even men of science know their limitations."

"Then your feelings about Easter and the Resurrection are a mixture of scepticism, uncertainty . . ."

"And a romantic spirit," he completed for her. "I told you I was a pagan, so how can you wonder that I should rejoice at the most lyrical of pagan feasts? My heart really does dance with the daffodils, I wish everybody well, and I should like everybody to be full of hope on this one day of the year. Above all, I should like you to be happy, Rose; your sky of a cloudless blue."

"I don't know why you should think otherwise, Gilbert; only because I confessed to my foolish nervous forebodings."

She remembered, however, not suddenly, because in Gilbert's company the thought was seldom far from her that he had been the recipient of Walter's confidences. He, and he alone, knew the condition upon which their marriage had been based. He was the third party to their secret; to *her* secret, rather, because she had long since decided that Walter, having arranged the matter to his own satisfaction with her connivance, had dismissed it from his mind as he would dismiss a business transaction once it had been signed and witnessed. A marriage contract of an unusual nature, whose execution had been left to her, with no further trouble to him. She was proud to feel that she had never given him any trouble, not in all these years, not even in the first difficult years, not even when they had gone off together on holiday to the warm Spanish islands where all the scents and the soft night air and the songs across the sea suggested sensuality and love; tortured though she had been by the desire to take his hand, to entice him towards her, to force him into breaking his vow of celibacy—was he a monk? And was she not his wife?—she had resisted. She had not failed him. A promise given must be a promise kept. A bargain made and honored.

Now that all that glory of struggle had subsided, she felt the poorer for her acquiescence. She had felt herself a more noble creature in the days when she had fought her desires, and conquered. Then, she was doing something for Walter, something that took all her strength; now, she was a broken thing, flaccid, empty. All the strength that she possessed, put into that struggle, had exhausted her. She had made her life's effort.

How much of all this did Gilbert know? How much did he guess?

৪৶

"Gilbert, you are fond of Walter, aren't you?"

"Need you ask me?"

"Yes, I know. . . . I sometimes think that people misunderstand Walter. They think him inhuman. Lawyers are obliged to be a bit inhuman, aren't they? They have to take an objective attitude towards their cases; and taking the objective attitude sometimes means that you must lose sight of the human side; I mean, you have to administer the law, and you can't take into consideration the personal case or hardship. Would you say, Gilbert, that Walter was especially harsh, as lawyers go?"

Gilbert hesitated as to what answer to give. The bird was approaching; it was prinking round, drawing nearer and nearer; it was on the verge of pecking a grain from the palm of his extended hand. He realised that Rose was asking a double question: was Walter a hard advocate, was Walter a hard man? He must be careful.

"Walter is highly regarded in his profession. In a difficult case, where the verdict was in doubt, Walter would be the man to employ."

"Regardless of his belief in the rights and wrongs of the case?"

"Rose, surely you have been married long enough to our leading Q.C. to know that the rights or wrongs of the case have nothing to do with it? It is a game of chess, no more. Walter plays a very good game of chess at home. He enjoys it. He gets an intellectual pleasure in scoring off me or any worthy opponent. Then he plays the same sort of game in the courts of justice."

"And all the people concerned are pawns or knights or castles or kings and queens to him? He moves his pieces; his adversary moves against him; he wins, he loses; if he wins, he has a moment of satisfaction; if he loses, he shrugs his shoulders and starts another game. Is that what you mean?"

"That is the way it works out, no doubt. A man has to be realistic in his profession. Competition is too urgent, our system of organisation too complex. No room for idealism or ideologies. The most one can hope for is integrity."

"Walter is noted for his integrity; he is not self-seeking."

Gilbert nearly said that it was not necessary to be self-seeking when one was supremely successful. One could afford oneself the luxury of a reputation for integrity when one was making ten, twenty thousand a year; but because Gilbert had generosity in his nature he said, as he truly believed, that Walter would always possess integrity, whatever his circumstances. He knew that Rose had based her life on pride in Walter, and on admiration for him, having little else on which to base it, and that she would greedily accept any tribute paid to him, so he added:

"Even if Walter were starving in a garret, he would never depart from his principles: he is the honest man."

"I sometimes wish, Gilbert, that Walter could have been compelled to starve in that garret at one time in his life. He would have learnt so much. He might even have taken a mistress to himself; a cheap little girl, fond of him, making no demands on his time, but patient and loving when he wanted her, even passionately loving in their rumpled broken-down bed. Thin young arms round his neck . . . And then when he had earned a few pounds, he would give her something extra to buy herself a pretty frock. He would have smiled down at her delight, with that irresistible smile of his."

"You draw a very vivid picture of their London-sparrow life."

Rose took no notice of his remark; she went on with what she was saying.

"I wish also that he could have suffered. Supposing, let us say, he had had a son; a son that he adored; killed in war, or by accident. Such things do happen to other people, but not to Walter. He is the lucky man. Everything goes right for him, and anyhow, would he ever have allowed himself to adore his son? I doubt it. He is too stern with himself. He has never allowed himself the luxury and the pain of loving beyond the point where you find it hard to manage your love. Yet one can imagine, can't one, Gilbert, a young man, Walter's son, in whom he took a pride and whose death would dash him? Don't let us say death only: let us say that that son did something utterly disgracing; something that Walter in his professional life would normally refuse to defend. Where would he find himself then? He would be torn between his emotions and his principles. . . . I must say," she said, blowing a smoke ring, "it would give me some amusement to watch Walter placed in a situation like that."

Gilbert noticed that she said "his son," not "our son."

"Perhaps Walter, like you, suffers from fear," he said. "Perhaps he is resolved on self-protection."

"You think that a sufficient reason for never allowing yourself to care for any human being in your life?"

"Come, Rose——"

"Don't say he cares for *me*," she said, making caps of her hands over her ears; "he is used to me, and might find it inconvenient to get on without me. No more. He doesn't care for me because he is not capable of caring; if ever there was a little spark of feeling in him, he put his heel on it long ago, as one stamps out a spark on the carpet. There are only two things he cares for: Svend and Anstey. If anything were to happen to either of those two things, his dog or his home, how would he take it? I just don't know, Gilbert. Isn't it strange, to have been married to someone all these years, and not to know how they would take a personal sorrow of that sort? His dog and his home . . . Svend and Anstey . . . Please don't think that I am criticising him. I cannot tell you how much I admire his sense of justice and the enormous compassion he has for people in their troubles. He seems able to understand everything, so long as it doesn't affect him or anyone close to him. I think perhaps no one realises, as I do, how deeply moved he is by any painful recital; his manner must be utterly misleading as he listens, and even I should have no inkling of the true effect had I not once or twice seen him at a moment when he did not intend to be seen. It was his anger that revealed him to me on those occasions. Fury with God and man; disgust with society. Rage that we had contrived to make such a hash of things; a desire to revenge himself on some unknown Power whom he might hold responsible. I really believe that if by touching a switch he could obliterate the whole of mankind, he would touch it. I have been frightened—such anger appals; and what makes it more terrible is that it is impersonal: cold, not hot. If it scorched me like a furnace, the furnace of a house on fire, I could bear it better; as it is, I feel I have been left naked on an ice floe in the Arctic. . . . It hasn't happened very often," she added with a smile.

"Your description is scarcely that of a passionless man."

"It is passion gone wrong, don't you see? It is the fallen

angel. The good angel in him is the pity for affliction and pain; the demon is the hatred for evil and futility. That makes him want to destroy. Cynicism would be a mild word."

Gilbert thought back over conversations he had had with his brother; they had been quiet discussions, as between adult men, but their general tenor inclined him to believe that Rose was indulging in no farfetched imaginings. Sometimes when he had wondered as to the extent of Walter's worldly ambitions, his cautious probings had drawn nothing but the revelation of a bleak contempt. Success was to be regarded as a bauble, gratifying enough if it came unsought to the hand, but on no account to be pursued or, when achieved, esteemed. This indifference was one of the things which caused Walter to be feared; not natural, it led to mistrust: what game was the fellow playing? It was not to be accepted at its face value. Gilbert, however, could understand it, for his own selfless profession predisposed him to the idea of service with no ulterior aim.

Rose, to his surprise, put his own thought into words.

"I think the only fundamental difference between you two brothers is that you, Gilbert, are all of a piece, whereas Walter is divided. Neither of you gives a damn for renown. You both work for the sake of your work; only, Walter works in bitterness and pessimism, and you work in mercy and hope. You are both practical men, you and Walter, but you, Gilbert, have something Christ-like about you, with all the demon in Walter left out. You must be the happier man."

"Rose, I never credited you with such a gift of analysis."

"Oh well," she said, getting up in her fidgety way off the arm of her chair to rearrange the illustrated papers on the central table. "Oh well, one does notice people, doesn't one? One learns what they are. It may take years, but after years one puts the picture together. Pieces fit. . . . There is seldom a piece that doesn't eventually fit. The picture begins to make sense. But we have talked seriously for long enough; wouldn't you like to come out?"

"Out," said Gilbert; "the fetish of the English. Out! A nice brisk walk. The remedy for all ills, whether of the soul or the body."

Rose laughed.

"You have given me quite a lot to think over, Gilbert, for one morning. And in any case, I hear Juliet; one always hears Juliet from a long way off—— Yes, darling!" she called back to Juliet on the landing upstairs. "We're down here; come and join us."

"I think I shall go for a walk by myself," said Gilbert in a hurried whisper. He found Lady Quarles somewhat overwhelming. "You see, Rose, you also have given me quite a lot to think over."

Chapter 9.

SUNDAY EVENING

"Walter? May I come in?"

"Gilbert! . . . Sorry, you startled me. Yes, of course, come in. Sit down, won't you? Here are some cigarettes, or do you prefer your pipe?"

Disturbed in his work, even as Juliet had disturbed him on the previous evening, he pushed his papers aside and fussed round to find an ash tray for his brother. Gilbert watched him with interest and amusement. Dear Walter! He could not bear to be jerked out of his routine. Neither could Svend, who was growling softly, a thick growl, right down in his throat.

"Shut up, Svend," said Walter. "Lie down. Sit."

Svend obeyed instantly, as always, flattening himself at

Walter's feet, quelled by a word. He obeyed, yet he continued to growl, secretly, to himself.

"He doesn't like you, Gilbert," said Walter. "I can't think why. He doesn't trust you. He trusts Juliet; she is his friend; he feels safe with her. He doesn't feel safe with you, Gilbert; he growls at you; it is odd how an animal, a dog, can tell the difference between the person he can trust or can't trust. Why doesn't he trust you? Why should he growl at you, my brother?"

"Does he trust you, Walter?" said Gilbert, looking at the dog.

"I think he does," said Walter, looking at Svend; "I think he does; I hope he does. If *he* doesn't trust me, then I don't know who would. If he betrayed me, I should indeed lose all my belief in love. If I betrayed him, he would indeed be justified in regarding me as a Judas. I should be giving him the traitor's kiss."

As though he knew what the two men were talking about, Svend got up and came to lay his nose across Walter's knee. He stood there, and Walter's hand caressed him.

ও

"He believes in you," Gilbert said, "as Christ's disciples believed in Him. Blindly? A matter of faith? Total faith? Unquestioning faith? Not a matter of Reason. You believe in Reason, don't you, Walter? You are a rational man, guided by Reason rather than by your emotions, even as I am. We are both rational men."

"Of course I believe in Reason," said Walter. "What else can one possibly believe in? If in that, indeed—— But what is all this leading up to? I cannot imagine that you have come merely in order to talk about my dog."

"Now be honest. What you mean is, why the hell do I come interrupting you in the sacred hours when you are working? Yes, I know that I am interrupting, and I know also how annoying it is to be interrupted; it is the unforgivable thing to do to a busy man. I, also, am usually a busy man. Therefore I can appreciate your resentment at my breaking into your private room in this way. But I am having an Easter holiday, remember, thanks to you and your charming wife, and you must allow me to enjoy a little fun of my own. Besides, I will ask you to believe me when I tell you that I have a very serious motive."

Walter stared at his brother.

"What is it you want of me?"

"I want to put your belief in Reason to the test."

Walter smiled; not his charming smile, but a rather supercilious, superior smile; unpleasing; almost a sardonic grin.

"I hope you will not find me lacking in my belief in Reason."

"Well, we shall see. I may be putting you to too severe a test. . . . I want Svend."

"Svend? *Svend?*"

"Yes, your dog. You see, you were mistaken for once; I did come merely in order to talk about your dog."

"I don't understand," said Walter. "What on earth do you mean by wanting Svend? What do you want him for? Why should you want him? He's *my* dog; you don't want a dog for yourself, do you? And if you do, why not buy one for yourself? He doesn't like you, anyhow."

"I want him," said Gilbert. "I need him."

Walter got up and walked up and down the room.

"You must be crazy," he said. "Look, I'll give you one of his puppies; I put him to stud four months ago; I didn't like the idea, but I thought it would be good for him; he's a virile young animal and I thought it unfair to thwart his natural instincts. He threw nine sons and two daughters to the bitch. Eleven in all. A fine proven sire. Pedigree puppies, and not a runt in the whole litter. I know they are not all sold yet. I could get one for you."

"I don't want a puppy," said Gilbert, thinking meanwhile how touching it was, this mixture of repugnance and boastfulness, and the little technical phrases that Walter had picked up from the kennel. A "proven sire"! The very word "proven" must have given Walter some satisfaction with its legal echo. Proud of Svend for his virility, yet Walter's twisted nature resented the physical copulation of his private, personal dog with an unknown bitch in heat. Besides, dogs after copulation looked so particularly ridiculous. Gilbert hoped, with a momentary softening towards his brother, whom he was nevertheless determined to hurt to the uttermost extent within his power, that Walter had not stood by to watch that comic, degrading sight.

"I don't want a puppy," he said. "I will take your word for it that they are fine, healthy puppies. It is Svend himself that I want."

"But why?" said Walter. "Why the hell?"

"Well, I will tell you," said Gilbert. "You won't like it, but I will tell you. I want him for experimental purposes. I have got a vitally important investigation in hand—an investigation which may lead to far-reaching results in our knowledge of the human brain. I won't bore you with details which in any case you wouldn't understand without specialised information such as I happen to possess. I will ask you only to accept my word for it. I and some of my colleagues are on the track of something quite as important as, let us say, the discovery of insulin in the treatment of diabetes, which, as you may remember, was the result of experiments on dogs, when Banting was enabled to isolate a certain sugar-absorbing substance given off by the pancreas. I instance insulin because that is the stock example which even ignoramuses like yourself have vaguely heard about. I could, of course, enlarge on my examples, but to a reasonable man like yourself it is scarcely necessary. You are no sentimentalist, Walter, to deny undeniable benefits. Why, dogs themselves have profited by experiments made on ferrets, a meaner animal, for the control of that ravaging disease, distemper. Your own Svend has been preserved from that danger. I presume that you had him inoculated at six months old by your local vet? Now if that meaner animal, the ferret, had not been sacrificed in the laboratory, your Svend might well have caught the disease and died away in misery, pain, and distress. You would not have enjoyed watching him, Walter, lying in a basket, covered over by blankets, his eyes streaming, his limbs twitching with something akin to St. Vitus' dance, and you knowing yourself without power to prevent or allay the trouble that had come upon him. Would you not then gladly have sacrificed a ferret, or dozens or hundreds of ferrets? Of course you would! The meaner animal must be sacrificed to the higher. The weaker to the stronger. That seems to be Nature's law. So if you admit that argument in principle, would you not also admit that the dog, as the meaner animal, should in certain cases be sacrificed to Man? If only you could see some of the miserable human beings that find their way into my consulting room, Walter, or into my clinic! Shuffling, shambling, mopping, and mowing, travesties of anything we believe a human being to be; subnormal beings; no hope to restore them to any normal functioning of the brain, unless . . . unless, Walter, I, your brother, find the solution, which is now very close to my hand. Think what a thing that would be. A discovery to be compared with the greatest discoveries of medical science: antiseptics, anaesthetics, prophylactics—a discovery which may revolutionise our whole knowledge of that strange complex instrument, the human brain! Think, Walter, of the enormous incalculable importance of the human brain. *Homo sapiens*. What has raised him above the rest of creation? Not brute strength; other animals were stronger than he. Not physical courage; other animals were as brave as he. Only the thinking man has lifted himself by his thought, by his brain. You may say, Walter, that by his brain he has contrived to make a sore mess and confusion of this small planet he was given to control. I would agree. But still you would not dispute that by man's brain alone can we hope for any ultimate solution of the problems which now appal us? Therefore, *ergo*, anything that I or my fellows can do to advance our understandings of the workings of the brain is to be encouraged. Yes? No?"

"Yes," said Walter, but he said it in a dead voice, with no more resonance of conviction than a muted string, a muffled bell.

"You agree? I thought you would. Well, then, having admitted the principle, you have only one step further to go. Let me have Svend for the advancement of this cause."

"For experimental purposes," said Walter. "You mean vivisection."

"That is what it is usually, though inaccurately, called."

"Well, you can damn well get some other dog," said Walter. "You're not going to have Svend for your horrible practices."

Always pale, he had now gone a grey-white. He sat down again, and his hand was trembling as he reached for a paper cutter and fidgeted with it.

"Oh, but consider," said Gilbert. "What is a dog? You can replace him. You could have one of those puppies you were talking about, Svend's son. If Svend died a natural death, you would replace him, wouldn't you? He is not the first dog you have had in your life, and no doubt he will not be the last. Within a month you would have forgotten him."

Walter said nothing.

"Whereas the benefit you would be conferring on me," Gilbert continued, "would be incalculable. And not on me only, but on thousands of sufferers for generations to come. You know very well that where pain is concerned you are an avowed humanitarian. You cannot bear the thought of it. If you were to see some of the people that I am compelled to see daily, their physical and mental anguish, the despair of those who love them and who have to be told that in the present state of our knowledge there is nothing, nothing to be done—if you were to see this, Walter, you would not hesitate over the immolation of a dog."

"Yes, I see that. Yes, Gilbert, I see what you must feel about it. But why Svend?"

"Why not some poor ownerless mongrel from the Battersea Dogs' Home? I will tell you why. For my experiment —and it may be the last I am ever obliged to make, so near am I to the final discovery—I require a dog of the highest intelligence, with a highly developed brain, you understand me. I have been watching your Svend for some time past, especially during these two or three days of your Easter party. I have observed him closely. Look at him now. He knows that something is afoot; he is uneasy; he is trying to understand what we are saying; he cannot understand; we are talking about something far beyond his comprehension. Yet his sensitivity tells him that something which he cannot understand is threatening his whole existence. Dogs are very interesting animals, Walter. They are interesting in the sense that, alone of the domestic animals, they have attached themselves to us and have adapted themselves to some of our ways. (I don't count cats; they are a thing apart.) But dogs! They will lie by our hearth, they will guard our home, they will give us devotion such as is seldom given by one of our own kind to another. No other animal has ever come so close to man, even to acquiring that ridiculous and wholly irrational instinct we dignify by the name of love. The dog has crawled down the centuries, creeping nearer and nearer on his belly, closer and closer towards his god and master, Man. Right down from the cave fire he has crept where once he snatched at a discarded bone—he must have been a primitive, wolflike creature in those days, with his cave man to match—a long journey until he reached his present

standard of development in that finished product you are
now stroking, Walter; you and your Svend; you so different
from your hirsute forebear in the cave, Svend so different
from the mangy snarling mongrel that once you kicked
aside but who still came creeping back to lick your hand.
. . . Do not let me draw too imaginative a picture. Let
me say only that even as you, Walter, have developed from
what your ancestor once was, so has Svend improved himself into exactly the highly developed type of dog I require.
Yes," said Gilbert, examining Svend with a professional
eye; "just what I want. Broad brow; plenty of space between the ears; a wide head; perfect! Couldn't be better.
You see, Walter, what I mean? Run your fingers over that
broad span. Feel his skull with your fingers; you will see
what I mean."

"I see," said Walter, his hand resting on the dog's head.
"I see what you mean. But it doesn't mean much to me,
Gilbert, what you are saying. You seem to be talking very
coldly about Svend. I don't think of him like that at all.
To me he is just Svend, my dog. You talk about him
objectively as a subject for experiment in your laboratory.
You are cold and brutal, Gilbert. I see that you have no
conception of what love and trust can mean."

"I talk coldly, do I?" said Gilbert. "Have you never
talked coldly yourself to clients who came to you in fierce
distress? Have you never met them with chilly, reasonable
arguments? Of course you have. So do I meet you now,
with reasonable argument to give up your dog. I want him,
Walter; I need him urgently. It is vital for me to have him.
I beseech you to believe me. I assure you that I am not asking this lightly. I urge you. I implore you."

Walter resumed his nervous pacing up and down the room. He was in torment. Gilbert watched him. He had got his brother exactly where he wanted to get him: on the rack. He meant to twist the screws as tight as they would go.

"But why Svend?" Walter said again. "Why my Svend?"

He ceased his walking; resumed his chair; and drew Svend again towards him, close, as though the two of them stood in alliance against the enemy.

"I told you," said Gilbert, driving home his persecution; "I told you why. He is the most intelligent dog I have come across; and, believe me, I have studied a good many. Svend excels them all. He has both the intelligence and the physique. He has the brainpan and the limbs. Look at him, Walter: he is superb, standing near you now, as you stroke him. Proud he is; a proud young creature. Three years old, isn't he? That would be twenty-one by a man's age. What a pity he isn't your son, Walter, instead of just your dog. If he were your son, you and Rose would be celebrating his coming of age this year. Three years old: yes, that is just the right age for my purpose."

"Gilbert, you are not serious; you cannot be serious; you can't really want him."

"But I certainly do, my dear Walter; I want him very seriously indeed. Do you suppose that I would come to you with this request if it were not of vital importance to me?"

"Gilbert, supposing I were to give him up to you, what would you do with him?"

"I see that you are hesitating; you are coming round to the idea of giving him into my hands. You want to know what I would do with him? Well, I would promise you not to hurt him more than necessary. You see, it would be only on his head that I should operate."

"His head," said Walter.

He looked down on that innocent head. Svend looked up at him with questioning eyes. Puzzled, he could not understand what was going on, but was willing, as always, to obey, to do what was asked of him.

"You would give him a general anaesthetic? He would not suffer? He would not know what was happening to him? Would he ever come round from the anaesthetic, Gilbert? Would he, in fact, survive the operation? No, I suppose not."

Gilbert wondered how far he might go in the torturing of Walter. How much would Walter stand? Supposing he were to say that no anaesthetic was possible? Supposing he were to describe exactly how the skull must be chiselled and chipped away to expose the living substance beneath? Supposing he were to describe Svend tied down to the operating table, secured by bonds round his body and his legs, so that he could not struggle against the things that men were doing to him? No, thought Gilbert; better not press Walter too far; not make the picture too vivid; not torment him beyond endurance, or he will revolt; he will not allow me to take his dog away. And at all costs, I must get his dog away from him; I must hurt Walter; I must bruise his heart; I must smash him; but I must not scare him to such an extent that I defeat my own aims.

"Of course he shall have a general anaesthetic," Gilbert said: "I promise you that. I won't let him suffer."

"But he will die?"

Gilbert shrugged.

"Probably. You would scarcely wish him to live, would you, afterwards? . . . Better for him to disappear. It will be in a good cause."

"You don't know what you are asking of me."

"Yes, I do know. I would not ask it if it were not of such high importance."

Walter hesitated.

"You don't know what he means to me."

"Yes, I do know, I tell you. You will say next that he is your only friend, the only recipient of your confidences. But that is sheer sentimentality, surely? A dog! You are talking like some old spinster crooning over her cat. Don't be so foolish. Be true to your own principles: Reason above all things. I told you at the beginning that I wanted to put your belief in Reason to the test."

"He is so beautiful," said Walter. He looked at the strong limbs, the glossy coat, the graceful attitude, the trusting eyes. "He is a handsome creature," he said piteously, appealing to Gilbert, the threatening enemy.

Gilbert, hardening himself, refused to respond to the appeal. He had to hit Walter as hard as he could. He had to scoff at any soft side betraying itself.

"My dear boy! Really! I didn't expect to hear this language from you. Beautiful! What is Beauty? A fortuitous combination of fur, muscle, and bone. If those limbs had been a little differently shaped, if the hairs in that coat of black and tan and silver had been a little differently arranged, if those eyes had been boot-button black instead of onyx, where would his beauty be then? Pure chance, aided by careful breeding. . . . Leave his beauty out of it. It is irrelevant."

"He loves me," said Walter.

After a pause he added, "And I love him."

Gilbert looked at his brother with a tenderness he hoped was not revealed through his eyes. Walter had put up no cogent argument; the Mortibois eloquence had not been brought into play; he had jerked out only a few stark phrases, more eloquent of himself than anything he had ever produced in the law courts. Gilbert, suffering himself almost as much as Walter suffered, loved him for it.

"My dear boy!" he said again. "First you drag in Beauty and then you drag in Love. You are talking all out of character. Those great vague words: beauty and love. Your voice indicated that you spelt them with capital letters. Yet, until this moment, I did not believe they existed in your vocabulary."

"They mean something," said Walter.

"I suppose they do. Poets and young lovers appear to have thought so. But I never associated you with poets or lovers. I always regarded you as the rational man, the adult man in the fullest sense of the term. You are failing me, Walter; you are allowing sentiment to creep in a swamp, a morass, between yourself and the clear waters of Reason."

"I'm sorry," said Walter. "I don't want to fail you. You are offering me a challenge I never anticipated. But I am afraid I must fail you all the same. It's no good, Gilbert, I can't do it. No man would. Neither your plea nor your ridicule can move me. You did shake me for one moment, but when it comes to the point I see that it is impossible."

Defeated, Gilbert had one more card in reserve. He respected his brother for the refusal; was, indeed, deeply glad; but he must push his stratagem to its cruel end.

"Very well," he said. "You now force me to tell you something I had intended to conceal. Within six months that dog will go blind. I have looked into his eyes, and I recognize the symptoms. Would you condemn him to such a fate? You would in any case see yourself obliged to have him destroyed. Would it not be better to lend what remains of his poor life for the immeasurable value I have suggested?"

Walter looked hard at Gilbert; then he looked down again into the trusting, questioning gaze.

"Are you sure?"

"Walter, I really do know what I am talking about."

"I can take your word, Gilbert? I would not believe anyone but you."

"You can take my word."

May God forgive me, Gilbert added to himself.

"This does rather alter the question," said Walter. "And you absolutely guarantee that he would not suffer?"

"I absolutely guarantee it."

"You seem to have cornered me. Very well, then: take him."

&⯈

Gilbert immediately became brisk and businesslike.

"Would you like a receipt for him? I have a form here."

"No, thanks," said Walter; "I don't want a receipt."

"He is a valuable dog, you know," said Gilbert, warning.

"No, thank you, I don't want a receipt."

"As you please. Now about his collar. I shan't need that. Would you take it off? It may come in useful for the next dog you get, perhaps for one of his puppies. I have a special collar here with me, with a metal label attached to it, which we like to have for all dogs designated for experimental purposes. I always travel with all this equipment, just in case I might need it."

"Come up here," said Walter.

Svend climbed up, laying his front paws across Walter's knees, in the familiar attitude. He felt safe there; proud and favoured.

Gilbert watched the trembling of Walter's hands as he unbuckled the collar and laid it on his table.

"Now put this one on."

He handed over a strong, rather shabby collar with a heavy metal disc dangling, stamped with a number.

"This has been used before," said Walter, looking at it with distaste.

"You can't expect me to supply a new one for every dog we use. Too many."

"I see it is the sort with a running noose—what they call a stranglehold."

"One likes to be on the safe side," said Gilbert.

Walter slipped it over Svend's head.

"Anything else?"

"Have you a lead for him?"

"He has never needed a lead."

"I thought you might say that. I took the precaution of bringing one."

Gilbert produced it from his pocket, a strong chain, rattling.

"Hook it into the collar, will you? As you remarked, he doesn't like me, and he might resent me handling him while he is resting across your knees."

Walter hooked it on.

"There is your prisoner," he said, "chained and numbered. Anything else?"

"Yes, there is something else. Have you a muzzle for him?"

"He has never needed a muzzle."

"Not even when he has travelled by train?"

"He has never travelled by train. He has never left Anstey since I first had him as a puppy, except when I have taken him to Scotland, and then we went together by car."

"I brought a muzzle," said Gilbert; "or rather a leather strap to put round his nose. That means that he can't open his jaws."

Walter had a moment of revolt, a final dying struggle. The insult was too great.

"You are not going to fasten that thing on to him?"

"Oh, all right," said Gilbert, restoring the strap to his pocket; "if you don't like it, I won't put it on till I get him to London. My kennel man, you understand, has a natural mistrust of Alsatians. He thinks them treacherous, and doesn't want to get bitten. You can't blame him. And he will be a complete stranger to Svend, and as Svend himself will be puzzled and bewildered, there might well be a clash of wills between them."

"You call that treacherous, do you? It seems to me a normal reaction."

"You hate me, don't you, Walter?"

"I don't know," said Walter; "I don't yet know. Anyhow, if you are going, I wish you would go. What is the use of prolonging this conversation? Go down, Svend," he said, pushing the dog off his knees. The chain clanked as it fell to the floor.

He picked up the end of it and handed it to Gilbert. "Please go," he said; "please go."

ဆ

"Hullo, Walter," said Rose, coming into the hall an hour later. "Ready for dinner?"

She looked round, playing the hostess.

"Juliet, Lucy, Dick, Robin," she said, ticking off her guests. "Where's Gilbert? Gone upstairs to wash?"

"Gilbert has had to go to London unexpectedly," said Walter. "He asked me to make his apologies."

"An urgent call?"

"I presume so," said Walter. "He went in a hurry."

"Poor Gilbert—who would be a doctor? No peace in your private life, not even over Easter. Still, I suppose it has its own reward."

"By sacrificing his own private life, he may be saving someone else's life tonight," said Lucy in her little sententious way.

"Fine chap, your brother," said Dick. "Fine profession. Never think of yourself. Makes us all look small."

"Well," said Rose, "I suppose we had better go in to dinner. We shall miss Gilbert. He is always such good company. Where is Svend, Walter? He will be wanting his dinner too."

"I can't think of Walter without Svend," chirped Lucy. "I always say Svend is Walter's shadow."

"Where is he, Walter?" said Rose.

"I must have shut him into my room by mistake," said Walter, pretending to glance round.

"Shall I get him, Uncle Walter?" said Robin, preparing to be helpful, and starting off towards the door.

"No!" said Walter in a suddenly loud voice which made them all jump. "Don't interfere, boy. If I shut him into my room, it was because I meant to. Let us go in to dinner. Juliet, you know the way."

Chapter 10.

MONDAY MORNING

Walter was not asleep. He had the impression of not having slept all night, though in fact he had dozed and been haunted by some horrible dreams. He had dreamt that he was given a lioness as a pet, but although her head was huge and hairy, in the normal way, she had no hide on her body, which was just raw red meat, sloppy when he patted it. He felt obliged to pat it, for she kept rubbing herself affectionately against his thighs, filling him with disgust, although he was ashamed of being disgusted and felt that he ought to be sorry for her and even fond of her.

He had woken then completely and lay for a moment wondering what had happened. Everything seemed so usual: the sun coming through the thin curtains, the bird song outside on this spring morning, his room in its accustomed aspect, his dressing table with his hairbrushes, the framed eighteenth-century prints of Anstey on the walls as he had seen it a thousand times. Then that disquieting sense of something wrong started to well up in him, but he had not yet remembered what it was. Then he remembered.

ह‌‌❧

He lay rigidly still, thinking. The lioness of nightmare had gone, leaving him to contemplate a far more horrible reality. He did not dare to move, lest the slightest physical motion should produce an onslaught of mental pain. He must remain numb for as long as possible. This was Easter Monday; Bank Holiday, when all the hard-working people would be out enjoying themselves on this lovely day which April was providing for them. His own garden, his renowned Anstey landscape garden, would be thrown open to the public; they would wander beside the lake, admiring; they would rejoice in the sheets of wild daffodil; they would peer into the grotto; the nymph's grotto, where he and Juliet had sat with Svend, listening to the drip of the water, while Juliet tore frond by frond from the ferns, telling him her sorrow about her son at a time when he, Walter, had no sorrows of his own and could not enter with his whole understanding into the desperation of another. The public would invade the garden, dropping their shillings one by one into the tin money box. They would have been politely requested at the entrance gate either to leave their dogs in their cars or else to keep them on the lead. This was not because Svend objected to strange dogs; on the contrary, he had a queer liking for making friends with every fresh carload of arrivals, and was always very much surprised and hurt if a visiting dog snarled at him. A born host, Rose always called him; the young host; the son of the house, she would say, having no son of her own.

Today, Svend would not be there.

ૐ

Walter lay still. A bumblebee came in through his window and blundered about his room. It was all very much the same as twenty-four hours earlier, when he and Svend were there together. The buzzing of the bee aroused his memory with special vividness: it was the moment of happiness made audible. He stirred, and a little moan escaped him, as though provoked by physical distress.

He looked at his wrist watch, which Rose had given him. Eight o'clock. At what hour, he wondered, did Gilbert start on his day's work? Bank Holiday would make no difference to that inexorable man. Was he, perhaps, already in his operating theatre, white-coated, ready to begin? This thought was too much for Walter; he sprang from his bed and hurried into his clothes.

He must face the day. Some explanation would become necessary, and he tried to think how best he could manage it. Last night he had contrived to impose submission on his guests, though whether he had done it by the initial violence of his manner or by his subsequent volubility at dinner and after dinner he neither knew nor cared. He had seen them looking at him, perplexed but intimidated, not daring to ask the question they wanted to ask. He grinned now to himself, thinking how peculiarly ill-adapted they all were to this enforced discretion: Juliet, who always said outright what was in her mind, an *enfant terrible* on occasion, profiting by her privilege of an adored and adorable woman; Lucy, always more full of curiosity than tact; Dick, a good old blunderhead, clumsy and well meaning; Robin, who had tried, poor boy, to be serviceable and had collapsed into silence after getting so alarmingly snubbed for his pains. Rose? Not a guest, but his wife, his hostess sitting at the opposite end of his dinner table. He had caught a glance from her between the little avenue of shaded candles, a glance not of enquiry but of concern: did she, then, care so much about anything which might be affecting him? They had lived such separate lives, always, meeting only on the surface for so many years, that it astonished him to encounter that anxious and loving gaze. Catching his eye, she had tried to smile at him, a smile of uncomprehending sympathy, but he had glanced away, turning to Juliet with some remark. He could trust Rose to protect him outwardly, but he would not allow her to make him the subject of private investigation. No such collusion should unite them; he must be alone. Defiant, he had addressed himself to the task of amusing his guests, remembering his own words to Svend by the lake in the morning to the effect that they could not have the day to themselves since they had to entertain an Easter party. He had spoken truer than he knew; and now, in a kind of fierce loyalty to Svend, he set out to entertain them by himself. Rose could not imagine what had seized him. Invariably courteous, he usually gave the impression of getting through the evening in a slightly absent-minded way, smiling so obligingly that his interlocutor was left wondering if he had any idea what he was smiling at, putting on so plausible a show of interest that people, deceived for the time being, wondered afterwards if he could in fact have been listening to their chatter at all. It was generally recognised, and tactfully arranged, that what Walter Mortibois really looked forward to was sitting down to the chessboard after dinner or getting into a corner with one or two men for a discussion that no one dared to interrupt. But that evening, to Rose's bewilderment, he laid himself out in a rare mood to display all the resources of his intelligence, experience, and wit. Walter could be the best of raconteurs when he liked. But why, she asked herself, should he suddenly elect to show off before that particular company? Juliet he was well used to; he would lazily pretend to flirt with her, accepting the convention that her extreme femininity exacted from all men; but their friendship was too old and calm and established for her presence to exercise any unusual stimulus. It was even less likely that he would wish to dazzle poor old Lucy or her Dick. (Robin he was certainly dazzling: the boy had never listened to such talk; Rose could see his awe and admiration of Uncle Walter growing with every fresh bit of toast he took to crumble.) What, then, possessed Walter? He kept them sitting for hours over the dinner table, he who was usually so impatient to move away; he kept them entertained by anecdote after anecdote, reminiscence after reminiscence, observation after observation, now laughing at his stories, now sobered by his wisdom, now laughing again, but always under the spell of his virtuosity. A wonderful performance. Rose, who thought that she knew something of him, came to the conclusion that she knew nothing at all. She knew only that something must have happened to him and that this was the defence he was putting up.

Sitting at the end of the table, confused between the soft light of the candles and the feverish fireworks of Walter's talk, she could find only one explanation. Something dreadful must have happened to Svend. He was, inexplicably, missing. The only break in the evening's entertainment was when Summers came in with the coffee tray and said, with the watchful familiarity of the old retainer:

"Svend hasn't cleared up his dinner, Sir Walter. Why, he hasn't touched it at all! And we got him a special bit of liver over Easter as a treat. . . . Why, he isn't in his corner," said Summers, looking about. "Would he have gone under the table? He sometimes does."

"He won't want his dinner tonight," Walter had said in the midst of a frightened hush. "You can take his bowl away."

ॐ

Now Walter was thinking how to get through the day. He wished he were alone with Rose, suddenly realising that Rose was the only person to whom he could bear to tell the truth. She would understand, and would assail him neither with questions nor with unendurable expressions of sympathy. She would merely look gravely at him and would say, "I see." She had always been like that, whenever he had been worried or preoccupied, never intruding upon him further than he desired. Dear, selfless Rose—the only woman to whom he could have borne to be married. Perhaps he had not always treated her with the consideration she deserved. Perhaps she, also, had a private life of which he knew nothing. If some real trouble had come upon them both, perhaps it would have brought them close together—not that he desired closeness to any human being, but Rose, he now thought, might have preferred it. There might, indeed, have been times when she wished to turn to him for counsel and comfort, but refrained, partly because she would not bother him and partly because she knew she would meet only with a conventional response. He could imagine himself glancing at the clock and saying, "Yes, my dear? I can give you half an hour before I have to go out."

Meanwhile, he, in his egoistic way, had built up throughout the years since their marriage a system by which he could depend upon her without cost to himself. The system had been started, according to his methodical, planned fashion, from the very moment he made his proposal to her in the Yorkshire wood: he had then invented the Rose he wanted, and she, compliantly, having once accepted his terms, had adapted herself to his invention. Had he, thereby, created a new personality, a person that was not the true Rose as nature intended? Pygmalion brought Galatea to life; had he, Walter, as a Pygmalion in reverse, destroyed the potential life in his Galatea?

That was a question that he must think out later. For the moment, the day was ahead of him, and, now that he had lost Svend, he had only Rose to turn to. She would protect him against Juliet, against Lucy and Dick, against Summers coming with Svend's bowl at luncheon; she would see to it that his torture was not increased.

ε∾

He found her, presently, putting things straight in the hall and looking as he was always accustomed to seeing her, fresh in her pretty clothes and surprisingly young in the sunny room amongst her flowers. He saw that she looked at him nervously, as though uncertain what to expect; well, he could not grudge her that. If he could have seen his own face, he would have respected her for repressing a start and for saying merely:

"Good morning, darling. A beautiful day!"

"Come into my room for a minute, will you?"

He shut the door behind them as on Saturday morning she and Gilbert had seen him shut it behind himself and Svend, and then seemed at a loss how to proceed. He saw her eyes roaming round, as though in search of some clue, and coming finally to rest on Svend's collar lying on the table. It retained the circular shape of the dog's neck. At that, she did give an exclamation.

"Walter, what has happened? Where is he? I think you really must tell me. It's not fair to leave me in ignorance any longer. It's not only this mystery about Svend; it's yourself; you look like death." Something impelled her to add, "Death in your heart," and her own heart shook with apprehension.

Walter picked up the rounded collar and examined it.

" 'My name is Svend,' " he read out. " 'Anstey Manor, Anstey.' You gave it to him, Rose, do you remember? You had it engraved for him when he was one year old."

He flung the collar from him into the furthest corner of the room.

"It was his only possession," he said. "He had nothing of his own. He won't need even this any more."

He sat down in his writing-table chair and hid his face in his hands.

"Walter!" cried Rose. She came round and knelt beside him. "Walter, my darling, for God's sake tell me what you mean. I would do anything for you—don't you know that? I would give my life to save you from one hour of misery—— Oh, don't push me away," she continued as he recovered his self-control and tried to get away from her. "Stay where you are," she said, holding him down; "stay where you are, and tell me. I love you, don't you see? I never say this sort of thing to you, because I know you don't want it, but it is all so true, so true. If you are in trouble now, won't you let me help you? Is Svend—dead?"

"I don't think so," said Walter in his coldest voice. "No, certainly not. Not yet."

"Not yet? Walter, please! You *must* explain."

"Let me get up, then."

She let him go, and he walked over towards the window, standing there with his back towards her, looking out. She remained kneeling beside his empty chair, broken by the impossibility of ever coming near to him. Her one poor effort had failed.

In the shortest, driest words he told her.

"Now what I will ask you to do for me," he said, "is to prevent anyone from asking me questions. I rely on you. I don't care what lies you invent to keep them quiet, only I don't want them to know the truth. That is a thing I could not endure. You can say, if you like, that I have sent him away to stud and that Gilbert kindly took him to London for me for that purpose. Yes, that will do."

"But, Walter, they will wonder why you didn't say so yourself last night when Robin offered to fetch him."

"Let them wonder. Let them think me odd, mad, anything they choose. Only stop them from mentioning the subject to me. For my part, I promise you that I will behave in a perfectly normal manner, appearing neither unduly depressed nor unduly elated. After all, we have to spend today and this evening with these people. One has obligations. We have to entertain our Easter party."

"It may help a little," she said timidly, "that the gardens will be open to the public this afternoon. Neighbours are sure to come over—neighbours who suspect nothing—and you can escape on the pretext of making yourself civil to them. If you can't be alone, as I am sure you would prefer, it is better to be with an indifferent crowd."

"Neighbours? The Reverend and Mrs. Pry from the Vicarage?" He changed his voice to a mincing accent, with the gift of mimicry that had often been used to such effect in cross-examination in the law courts. " 'And what have you done with your lovely dog today, Sir Walter? I always say to the Vicar, that dog is Sir Walter's shadow, don't I, dear?' As your sister Lucy said last night."

"Walter, *please.* . . . For God's sake spare yourself— and spare me," she added inaudibly, still kneeling on the floor beside his empty chair; but that was a plea she must not let him hear. She stood up. "Let us be practical," she said, straightening a ruler on his desk, putting the pile of quarto paper square, looking to see if he had enough envelopes in his stationery cabinet—all quite unnecessary, since Walter's table was always a model of tidiness.

"Let us be practical," she said again. "I promise to invent something to keep them all quiet."

He was still standing over by the window, his back turned towards her.

"Thank you, Rose," he said. "I knew I could depend on you. I wish I were alone with you today."

She had her reward.

ह

The neighbourhood spent a very pleasant afternoon strolling round the lake at Anstey on this perfect April day. They came in private cars and in coaches, on bicycles and on foot, not the neighbourhood only, but people from a distance, and all said how fortunate Sir Walter and Lady Mortibois were in having so beautiful a home. Perhaps there was a touch of envy in the thought that on ordinary days they could stroll at their leisure with no crowds to mar their enjoyment. Anstey had two seasons of extreme beauty, one in spring and the other in autumn. In spring the lake lay cupped under the amphitheatre of high banks where the beeches rose tier above tier in all the freshness of their young green, and on the slopes of grass going down to the water the daffodils blew in their yellow myriads, varied by sheets of the blue anemone, naturalised, sowing itself so recklessly that it cropped up even between the cracks of the paved floors in the temples, little tufts of azure pressed against the foot of a column, as it might be in Greece. That was half the charm of Anstey; that in spite of the grandeur of its design, the tall trees and the lowly flowers appeared to have come there of their own accord, completing the schemes of man. Even Walter sometimes found it difficult to believe that his ancestor had deliberately planted the beeches as a background to the lake and the temples, or had controlled a river for the formation of the lake itself.

This was Anstey in spring, but in autumn the colours changed from green, yellow, and blue to a warm symphony of brown and red. Brown on the beeches, red in the dogwood, foxy in the bracken; Anstey flew two differently coloured flags to match the seasons. Walter had always preferred the rich melancholy of the autumn. Today he almost hated the young leaves and the gay flowers, and to escape the laughter he took Dick off for a round of golf.

Lucy, somewhat disconsolate without Dick to talk to—Rose seemed to have disappeared—walked up and down a long gravel path and watched the people streaming down towards the lake. The path where she walked behind the house was roped off from the public, giving Lucy an agreeable sense of superiority. It showed that she was an inmate. A gardener on duty touched his cap to her. Slightly flustered by this, she made her next turn before she could reach the gardener; it would be ridiculous if she had to say, "Good afternoon," to him every time she passed. Lucy, besides watching the people, was thinking deeply, having more food for thought than had ever been vouchsafed her. Ever since she arrived at Anstey she had been working round to the conviction that something was wrong, a conviction which had been amply confirmed on Sunday evening by Walter's extraordinary behaviour, and again in the morning by an equally extraordinary conversation she had had with Rose. Lucy was quite sure now that one of her suspicions was correct: Walter was having an affair with Juliet. Had she not seen them wandering off together on Saturday evening towards the lake at that romantic hour between tea and dinner—the best they could do for themselves, no doubt, since not even so brazen a flirt as Lady

Quarles would dare to carry him off by moonlight *after* dinner—and had she not even then, watching from a window, drawn her own conclusions? The idea of Dick slipping away like that with another woman! Undoubtedly, her instinct had once more guided her aright. Her belief in her instinct, originally somewhat diffident and unformulated, had throughout the years been reinforced by Dick's often repeated remark, "Well, Pudding, you may not set up to be very brainy, thank the Lord, but you *have* got what's called feminine intuition, and no mistake." Her feminine intuition, strengthened by her Rectory love for her sister, could surely not have been at fault on this occasion. Nothing else could explain the evasiveness of Rose's manner, as though she, usually so self-possessed, were striving to confide some painful secret to her sister and found herself incapable of coming to the point. Lucy, grieved but nevertheless aware of some delectable titillation, decided to help.

"I know, Rosie," she said. "You needn't tell me. It's that Lady Quarles, isn't it?"

Rose had stared at her and then, to Lucy's stupefaction, had gone off into peals of laughter. But she had not denied it.

Lucy was sincerely shocked. Such levity, even though it might be assumed in order to hide a breaking heart, was most unbecoming and not at all in accordance with what should have culminated in a tearful sisterly confidence. Even expressions of the tenderest sympathy appeared only to increase Rose's amusement. If this was the way people of the Anstey world behaved over such serious, fundamental matters, then the sooner she and Dick went back to

Ontibon Street the better, taking their clean, guileless Robin with them. She drew away from Rose at last, having been foiled in her attempt to fold her sister to her bosom.

"I must say," she said with dignity, "I think that your sense of humour is exceedingly misplaced."

She had gone off and poured it all out to Dick, who said only that he wouldn't be at all surprised.

Lucy therefore found herself in a most unsettled state of mind as she paced up and down the path. On the one hand she was genuinely sorry for Rose, but on the other hand she had been cheated of a talk she would greatly have enjoyed. Such revelations might have been forthcoming, such details, such peeps into the wicked way of life! Walter had always been a bit of a mystery, and here, if ever, was the opportunity to uncover certain aspects of that enigmatic man. Although she had never been at her ease with Walter, and had recurrently speculated on the satisfactory or unsatisfactory nature of his relationship with her dear Rosie, she had always regarded him, the great lawyer, with awed respect as a guardian of public morality. The discovery, as she now thought, that his own morals were not of a kind to stand the light of exposure provided so painfully pleasurable an idea to Lucy that she scarcely knew, pacing up and down her path, how to cope with it. Her sparrow brain was matching itself against hawks, the hawks that hovered always above the woods of Anstey, poised ready to sweep on the mouse in the grass, the innocent life, to eat and destroy and corrupt it.

ह్

Just as Lucy, trying to sort out the confusion of ideas into which Rose's well-intentioned Easter party had pre-

cipitated her, was watching the happy Bank Holiday public pouring into Walter's garden, she observed a couple
strolling by themselves apart from the main stream. They
strolled, not following the orthodox way, as though they
knew the short cuts and were inmates of the place, even as
Lucy herself was temporarily an inmate. She recognised
her own Robin walking with Juliet Quarles. Poor Lucy on
her straight path, pacing up and down, instantly feared the
worst for her child. That Lady Quarles, with all her charm,
who had brought trouble into Rose's life! She must not
bring trouble also into Robin's. Lucy felt inclined to act
like a hen partridge, pretending to trail a broken wing to
divert attention from her brood.

ﺝﻭ

Robin would have resented any such management on
the part of his mother. He was enjoying his Easter. He
liked his aunt Rose, who was so pretty and so amiable and
made everything so easy; and he had developed a cult for
his uncle Walter, who was so brilliantly clever and yet so
remote. Robin admired him, secretly deciding to model
himself on Uncle Walter's aloof manner in after years
when he, Robin, had attained sufficient eminence, as he
supposed he must. He had not much ambition for himself;
he had not wanted to go into the Colonial Service; he had
wanted to become an architect, but his father would not
hear of it; so now, Robin supposed, he must end up as a
colonial governor with a K.B.E., a prospect which had no
attraction for him at all. He wished he could talk to his
uncle Walter about it; he had looked forward to this
chance of consulting that wise man; but for some reason

his uncle Walter had suddenly become inaccessible, as though some accident had befallen him; he looked like someone who has been knocked down by a lorry and picked himself up again, bravely, but shaken, pretending to resume life as normal, an unconvincing bluff to any loving observer, as Robin was now.

There were things about himself he could have told his uncle, which he could not possibly tell his mother—he smiled at the very thought—or even his father; problems which beset his young life. He knew that his mother longed for him to marry, and would watch him with a kind of panting anxiety throughout his four months' leave, not saying anything outright, but dropping little hints, and always, when he came home after a party—and she insisted on sitting up to wait for his return, a fond habit which maddened him, but he must be kind to her—with a question in her eyes. He knew well enough what lay behind that question: had he met any nice girls? Robin did not like girls, however nice. Women did not attract him; that was the trouble. He greatly preferred the company of his own sex, and was instantly at ease with any man, especially elderly men, who always took a liking to him, usually far in excess of anything Robin was prepared to welcome. There had been unpleasant incidents with which Robin, less innocent than Lucy sweetly supposed, was by now quite competent to deal. But there were also his own inclinations, which worried him far more, as he had not yet learnt how to manage them.

He had discovered, however, that he liked Lady Quarles very much indeed. She might be all the things his mother said she was—irresponsible, unstable, intemperate, and a silly chatterer—but he suspected that under all these things she possessed a warm heart and a fund of sad sagacity. If only he knew her better, he could talk very genuinely with her, for she would surely understand the most fleeting allusions and would never indiscreetly insist. Alas, she was not likely, this spoilt and experienced woman, to take any interest in a boy like him.

Yet she had invited him to come for a stroll with her, down to the lake.

&

"You know," she was saying, "my Micky is just your age."

He envied her Micky, but, being shy, could think of nothing better to say than:

"What does he do?"

"Gets into mischief mostly," said Juliet. "Your uncle Walter gives me good advice about him."

"I'm sure he does," said Robin warmly. "He's a wonderful person, isn't he? Lady Quarles . . ."

"What?" said Juliet as he hesitated.

"I'm not sure if I ought to say this."

"I won't repeat it."

"Well, then, what was the matter with Uncle Walter last night?"

"I don't know, Robin," she said gravely, "and I am not going to ask."

"No. No, of course not. But there was something, wasn't there? And today he looks frightfully ill; haggard, as though he hadn't slept. And at luncheon, although he was trying to appear as usual, he kept on getting absent-minded and staring in front of him as though he was seeing something that wasn't there. I did wonder if it had something to do with Svend, but it can't be that because Aunt Rose said Svend had been sent away for a couple of days to stud."

Juliet, to whom the same explanation had been given, was speaking the truth when she said she did not know. Rose's manner had been curt, almost offhand, on the defensive, and Juliet had respected her disinclination. She had had a few words with Walter, who had said only that on thinking Micky's case over he had decided to do all he could for the boy, and was sorry if he had seemed unsympathetic during their talk in the grotto.

"A bad habit of mine, I'm afraid," he said, "to look only at the facts and forget the human element. I should like to say now, dear Juliet, that I do feel very deeply for you in your anxiety about your son. It is cruel indeed to suffer anxiety on behalf of any beloved creature. I would beg you to believe that I am not so obtuse as I may sometimes appear."

Juliet was much surprised by this somewhat pompous little speech, and even more surprised by its evident sincerity. She squeezed Walter's arm as she thanked him, but did not say much, as he had most unexpectedly brought tears to her eyes. Micky was very dear to her, and she often lay awake wondering what would happen to him after she was gone. For she knew what none of her friends knew—that she had at most a year to live.

Chapter 11.

MONDAY NIGHT

The dreadful day passed; the crowds cleared off; the gates were shut behind the last stragglers; Anstey returned to its seclusion though not to solitude. Rose, encountering Walter in the hall, said, "Well, they've all gone," to be met by the gloomy reply, "Not all." No, it was true, they still had their guests; and, emboldened by the memory of his remark in the morning, she went close to him and said in a low voice, "I wish we were alone, darling."

"I wish to God we were," he replied, wringing her heart by the misery in his voice but rejoicing her at the same time by the fervour with which the words were spoken. He wanted to be with her and with her only.

They had met at intervals throughout the day; indeed it

seemed to Rose that he had deliberately sought to approach her, as though he derived some dumb comfort from her proximity. After all, they two were the only ones in the small company to know the truth; they shared a secret, and the sharing conferred on them the virtue of an alliance. When she had caught his eye at luncheon, and had smiled to him, he had smiled back; a sad smile, but at least he had not repudiated her. Rose, in anguish for him, was finding a terrible happiness in their unity. Far too timid after her long years of discipline to venture on any loving expression, she trusted, nay, she prayed that her unspoken participation might find its way into his hurt heart no less than if she could have taken his hand or put her arms about him. There was, in fact, she thought, something rather fine and proud in the strange bond that secretly held them together that day, finer than anything known to Dick and Lucy, for all their placid intimacy.

ॐ

The day had passed off without incident. No stranger, dropping in to tea, could have become aware of anything amiss. Rose, as it happened, thinking to submerge any possible gaffe on the part of Lucy—Juliet she could trust, Robin was too much overawed, and Dick simply did not count—had brought in several chosen visitors with the offer of tea; Colonel and Mrs. Cowley, Mr. and Mrs. Linley, the Vicar and Mrs. Pry. The inclusion of the vicar and his lady was partly mischief on Rose's part: she knew with what disapproval she and Walter must be regarded at the Vicarage, yet she knew also that when there was any question of funds to be raised for a local charity, or of a garden to be borrowed for a money-making fete, the sins and omissions of the owners of Anstey would be overlooked. (It gave Rose some pleasure to feel that she and Walter should thus be jointly regarded as the owners of Anstey.) Besides, the vicar, who in his home life was restricted to the most jejune and watery form of English fare, but who would have been a well-living man had his spouse and his vocation permitted it, was never proof against the buttery scones of the Anstey tea table.

"Thank you, Lady Mortibois, thank you! Yes, I think I might allow myself a second helping. After all, we have just celebrated the great feast of the Resurrection, have we not? Lent, with its mortifications, is happily over. Another scone—yes, thank you so much. Most delicious, if I may say so. Most delicious. Of course you have your Home Farm and your homemade butter. Such a difference! Such a difference with that insipid thing which the ladies call, I believe, Marj."

"Arthur!" said Mrs. Pry in an ominous voice. "Arthur, remember your figure."

For the first time that day a wave of natural amusement came over the house party. Juliet looked at Robin, and winked. Walter himself bent forward and, addressing himself to Mrs. Pry, said, with the utmost suavity:

"Are you quite sure it is his figure you mean and not his soul?"

Mrs. Pry did not know how to take this remark. Sir Walter was a great man, or so everybody told her, and he certainly possessed great charm of manner—that curious voice of his, so deep, slurring the r's—but she was not the woman to be carried away by external charm, and she had the profoundest suspicion of anything she might regard as sarcasm.

"The vicar is getting very plump," she replied with dignity.

&

Rose congratulated herself in importing these outside elements to break the strain of the day. When they had all taken their departure, having been seen off by Walter and herself waving good-bye from the top of the steps, the little house party was able to gather again in the hall and laugh together over the ruins of the tea table. Robin in particular caused much hilarity by his imitation of the Vicar and Mrs. Pry: the boy had a real gift of mimicry. Stimulated by Juliet's appreciation and by a grin from his uncle Walter, he excelled himself. Lucy beamed with pride. Dick popped at his pipe and said, "Ha! Ha!" every now and again. Rose was enormously relieved; she knew that all this gaiety was false and could only be temporary, but at least it was a respite and would get them through some moments of the remaining hours. After all, that was the way one usually lived: getting through some more moments of the remaining hours.

&

It could not last, as she had known it could not last. Juliet's laughter was still pealing out when Summers came in.

"Dr. Mortibois would like to speak to you on the telephone, Sir Walter. I have switched it through to your room."

Rose felt as if she had been shot. She looked at Walter, and he looked back at her. Then he went into his room, shutting the door behind him.

৯১

She saw him for a moment before dinner.
"Walter?"
"What?" he said roughly.
"Walter, please tell me. What did Gilbert say?"
He looked at her as though he could murder her; then he softened. She was his only friend; and he had made great demands upon her.
"It's all over," he said. "It was good of Gilbert to let me know."

৯১

If Rose hoped against experience that Walter would seek her in her room that night before going to bed, she was destined to disappointment. How she longed for him to come she would not admit even to herself, but with every creak of a board or closing of a door her heart turned over lest it might be he on his way towards her. She had despatched her good nights to Juliet and to Lucy with all the celerity conformable to good manners; Juliet, quick and sensitive, had let her go after one kiss, had almost pushed her out of the room; Lucy, heavy and sentimental, would have liked her to linger for one last, long talk while Dick still sat smoking and drinking downstairs, but on this occasion Rose was more than a match for Lucy. She must be tired, Rose said, making a show of concern; tired after a long day in the open air to which she was not accustomed;

country air was so much stronger than London's; and there had been all those people wandering about, enough to distract anybody, besides people to tea and that very harrowing thriller on the television after dinner. Lucy must certainly go straight to bed! She was not to hurry away in the morning, Rose said, knowing well that Walter would leave by car after an early breakfast; she must not dream of going before luncheon; they would pick some flowers together for Lucy to take back to Ontibon Street, and there would be some eggs and some butter. With all these promises she cajoled her sister into releasing her; embraced her affectionately, and left. To her relief, she saw Dick mounting the stairs; that meant that Walter had broken up the masculine party downstairs and would himself shortly be coming up to bed. He would rake the ashes over the fire, see that the front door was locked, and turn out the lights in the hall.

"Good night, Dick!" she called. "Good night, Robin!"

ह৯

Safe in her room, she waited, frightened by the beating of her heart. She could not bear to think of what Walter must be feeling: Was he numb now? Was he relieved, as one is relieved in a way by the finality of the inevitable? Had he gone through so much, in imagination, as to what might be happening hour by hour, that he could no longer register any sensation but an extreme weariness? If only he would come, that she might judge for herself! She did not know what she would dare to say to him; she must leave that guidance in his hands. She knew only that all the love she had so painfully suffered for him, crushed down, had reached its selfless culmination this day when she saw him hurt and could do nothing—or so little—to help him. Words, she thought, would be useless; nothing but a silent, physical contact of the utmost tenderness could unite them. If only—the longing was simple and elementary—if only she could hold him and rock him to sleep! Then she laughed to herself, a bitter little laugh: Walter, especially Walter in pain, was not the sort to let himself be rocked to sleep by any woman.

She did not know whether to undress or not or how long to wait before she finally gave up all hope of his coming. It was the measure of their separateness that it never occurred to her to go and look for him. She walked about her room, making those nervous little adjustments which were natural to her: a picture straightened, a hairbrush changed over to another place. She went into her bathroom, took off her dress, and wrapped herself in a blue silk dressing gown, deliberately dawdling. She put her dress on to a hanger, slowly, carefully, spinning out the minutes, and hung it up in the cupboard. Then she sat down before her mirror and brushed her hair, that glossy dark hair with the white quiff. She could not help admiring the lovely kink of the wave just beside the temple. Still Walter had not come, and still she had not heard him go to his room, but that perhaps was not to be wondered at, since his room was at the other end of the passage and the floor was thickly carpeted. "Oh, Svend!" she thought. "How your nails used to click on the parquet of the hall downstairs!" This stirred her again to an intense realisation of Walter: it was like being inside his mind. Cautiously she opened the door and peered out onto the landing; all was dark; the house was silent. The house held its secrets. Walter must have come up without her hearing him. She tiptoed forward and looked over the bannister down into the hall; nothing was to be discerned save the last glow of the embers on the hearth. For once, Walter must have neglected to pile up the ashes, but it was quite safe, the fire had nearly burnt itself out. Feeling as though she too had burnt herself out into a state of exhaustion, she returned to her room and went to bed since there seemed to be nothing else that she could usefully do.

ಕಿ

She did not sleep; it was scarcely to be expected. She lay trying to go to sleep, attempting every device, saying the alphabet backwards, repeating nursery rhymes in a sort of incantation, turning her pillow over to get the cooler side; she even got up to look out of the window at the moonlight shedding its unreal sheen over the grass, and at one planet infinitely serene, imperceptibly moving across the moonlit sky. "No, of course!" thought Rose. "It is the moon that moves more quickly in relation to the planet, even as the scudding clouds delude us into believing that the moon moves rapidly: an optical illusion." Walter, amongst his many other interests, included an interest in astronomy, not amateurish, but well informed. She remembered how on their honeymoon, spent in the Azores, he had taken her out on to the terrace of their hotel, and had pointed out the visible constellations and had given her what amounted to a lecture or a discourse on the movements of celestial bodies. Not for nothing had he been elected a Fellow of the Royal Society; he knew what he was talking about. He had poured out the treasures of his knowledge to his young

bride, seeking to interest her, since he conscientiously felt
an obligation to entertain this girl whom he had carried off
from her Rectory and who was now his wife, though less
his wife than his guest. If he denied her the fulfillment of
life in one direction, he must make it up to her in another;
and indeed he had succeeded in interesting her, unaccustomed as she was to this sort of talk in her Rectory home
or at the local tennis parties she attended. Lying awake,
she remembered all this, and how fascinated she had been
by Walter, and how proud and astonished she felt that this
exceptional man should be her husband, giving her a claim
on him. All the same, the mysteries of outer space seemed
a rather chilly topic to a young woman very much in love;
the celestial bodies were a very poor substitute for her own
urgent young body; and nothing but the resolutions she
had taken, which amounted to a marriage vow albeit of a
somewhat unusual kind, had prevented her in the air of
the scented southern night from obeying her natural instinct and from attempting—oh, most lovingly, most insinu-
atingly—to seduce him. "Sir, I will give you the keys of my
heart." Ah, she had already given them, but before hand-
ing them over she had deliberately turned them in the lock.
If he wished to use them, he was at liberty to do so; meanwhile, they were no longer in her keeping.

He had never, in all these years, chosen to use them.

ॐ

She lay awake, remembering other things that she had
thought forgotten. Small surprises that the incalculable
Walter had sprung upon her. In her humility, she had sub-
jugated herself to all his whims, all his queernesses, immo-

lating herself on the altar she had voluntarily and willingly erected. She now recalled a day when she and he, that honeymoon couple, had been wandering up one of the stony, terraced paths of the island, between the vineyards, and had come upon a peasant ill-treating his donkey. He was screwing its tail and jabbing the point of an aloe into its most sensitive parts. Walter, her cold detached Walter, had suddenly been transformed into a creature of hot rage. He had fallen upon the peasant, telling him in terms that Rose had never heard before, exactly what he thought of him and would like to do to him.

"I should like," Walter had said, "to kick you with hobnailed boots in the balls."

As he had spoken in English, it seemed unlikely that the peasant had understood anything except the unaccountable violence suddenly displayed by this member of a race reputed to be phlegmatic. His mouth fell open; he gaped. He was frightened for the moment; but as soon as the crazy Englishman had turned his back, he would go on treating his donkey as before.

She remembered also another day when on their wanderings they had come on a puppy lying in a ditch. It must have been hit by a passing car, and have crawled to its death where they found it. Walter gathered it up, so gently, so expertly with his delicate hands; it whimpered a little, but seemed to trust him. "No," said Walter, caressing it, handling it, "I won't hurt you more than I need." He had carried it back to the hotel, procured a box and some straw for it to lie on, to the astonishment of the hotel manager, who would have bashed the brains out of the little object with one heavy stamp of his heel; but the Englishman spoke with authority not to be refused.

Walter had put the broken leg into a splint, and had thereafter cared for the waif, devoting the rest of their honeymoon to its restoration to life and health. Every two hours, he said, he must go back to look after his puppy. The puppy recovered and ended by biting Walter rather sharply in the finger. Rose put on a poultice at his request; that, at least, was something she could do for him.

Baffling mixture that he was, so tender to the little mongrel, so cruel towards herself! He must surely have known how cruel he was being, or had he succeeded in atrophying his own impulses to such an extent that he had ceased to remember they might still potently exist in somebody else? Rose herself had almost forgotten the thwarted flashes of her early love for him: she had stamped too effectively on their fires. Those nights in the Azores, those honeymoon nights, were now so far and long ago, they had faded away with all her hopes, her dreams. It had been warm there; she remembered how warm the air had been; she and Walter could stand out on the balcony, without coats, looking up at the stars, and not a shiver of terrestrial chill coming over them.

That was a warmth of temperature seldom known in England. This single April day at Anstey, this day after the Easter Resurrection, had been warm enough, sunny enough, to please the meek long-suffering population of a northern island. They could not, and did not, expect such dulcet weather to last for more than twenty-four hours. Fully and resignedly they anticipated a change for the worse, which might arrive at any moment. Rose, lying sleepless, heard it arrive at midnight. She heard the wind blow up, after the breathless day, getting up in such force as to rattle the window panes and even shake the house. It was a gale, such as arises in the hours of darkness, when most people are abed and asleep and unaware, except for the sorrowful, the sufferers, and those at sea.

ε➷

Towards one o'clock in the morning, Rose, still awake, still vainly seeking sleep, the one desired oblivion, detected a peculiar smell coming into her bedroom. She sat up in bed, sniffing. A smell of smoke . . . She got up, switched on the light, put on her dressing gown, and opened her door. A volume of smoke greeted her on the landing. She ran quickly along the passage and found Walter's door.

"Walter!" she said. "Walter! I think the house is on fire."

He was in bed, reading by a bedside lamp. Tonight, it was Donne's sermons that he was reading, unguent to his wounds:

You add earth to earth in new purchases, and measure not only by acres but by manors, not by manors but by shires. And there is a little quillet, a little close worth all these, a quiet grave.

It was so long since she had seen him in that intimate, private way, that she stood on the threshold of his bedroom, hesitating to go in, despite the urgency. Yet he was the only person she could go to when their home was burning down.

He looked up, startled.

"Rose? What was that you said?"

"The house is on fire. You must get up; you must come.

We must do something about it. Come quickly. Nobody knows about it except you and me." Even at that moment it gave her some pleasure to pronounce those words. "Perhaps we may be able to put it out, between us, without alarming anybody else. There are fire extinguishers everywhere. Only do please come quickly."

He leapt from his bed, and together they went out on to the landing, smoke rising in great grey columns towards them.

"Rose. This is something serious. Go back into your room and telephone for the fire brigade. Lose no time. Put on some clothes, take anything you value, and go down by the back stairs. Don't attempt this staircase: you will be suffocated. I will rouse the others. Hurry."

ào

Within ten minutes they were all standing out at the front of the house, watching the smoke, shot here and there with a tongue of flame, pouring from the windows of the hall. The wind was high, a rough angry wind, blowing the smoke hither and thither, catching it and tossing it about, in great grey and black scarves slashed with the red of fire. The curtains of the hall suddenly billowed out through the broken glass, blood-red flags streaming on the gale. It was a fine sight, a grand sight; magnificence in destruction. Rose looked at Walter, to see how he was taking it. She had never seen so exalted an expression on his face before. He stood there, watching, the red of the flames putting a flush of colour on to his granite face and sending shots of scarlet across his grey hair. He seemed transformed, a different man, a man suffering a violent form of catharsis, a purging, an experience; and in his exaltation he made all the group around him look very small and dingy.

ॐ

Rose, looking round at them in that curiously detached way that sometimes occurs in the midst of a major catastrophe, when nothing seems real, like being in the calm centre of a cyclone where birds fly happily and sing—Rose observed her companions in disaster, her Easter party thus altered and disrupted. It was at the women she looked first. Juliet, lacking all her make-up, appeared suddenly aged and raddled and alarmingly ill, as she stood clutching a small attaché case and trying to hold her fur coat round her while the wind shrieked and sought to tear it open, out of her grasp. Rose noticed that she had put on a pair of stockings, which were now coming down in wrinkles round her ankles. There was something grotesque in this vision of the lovely Juliet, who in her daylight mood still put up so good a pretence of almost youthful charm: it was an outrage that she should stand so revealed. She had, it was true, in one desperate effort at seemliness, tied a silk scarf round her head so that at least her hair should not blow in maenad disorder; that was the only tribute to vanity she had found time for; Walter, calling her from her room, must have chivvied and hustled her. Lucy, on the other hand, looked very much the same as usual. Her face, habitually innocent of cosmetics, showed no startling change: she had few secrets to conceal. Even the old raincoat she had dragged round her shoulders might have been her customary wear in the country, as indeed it was:

stained, and serviceable, with huge pockets. It might equally well have belonged to Dick or to her. Her hair blew about, but then her hair always did blow about. Lucy scored over Juliet, exposed to this test.

ह

Rose then looked at the men. Walter she had already observed, and that one glance had given her a shock of excitement such as she had seldom experienced. She must put that moment of shock aside, to be considered later when this extraordinary event of Anstey burning was over and done with. She could not yet credit so unexpected an occurrence; she could not believe that Anstey would burn to the ground and nothing be left. The fire brigade would come, with huge pythons of hose pipes and helmeted young men leaping with axes off their scarlet dragon to cope with the triple elements of fire, wind, and water. Anstey would be damaged, but surely saved.

Dick, in his aquascutum, stood foursquare; he seemed solid and reliable, just waiting to be told how to make himself useful. Robin would play up, she felt sure, less from inclination than from devotion to Walter; he stood there, never taking his eyes off Walter's face. In his young handsomeness, he suddenly reminded her of Svend, waiting to jump to Walter's word of command, but there was a softness about Robin, she now realised; a softness which had no counterpart in the unequivocal strength of the dog. So much for Robin. Poor old Summers was shuffling incompetently round; this was something entirely outside his training as a butler, entirely removed from the careful carrying of tea trays or the setting out of fine glass and china for dinner on the brown mirror of a mahogany table. Such gentle, futile, civilised occupations, circumscribing the frontiers of Summers' life! No wonder he indulged himself, ludicrously and incongruously, in theoretical dreams of a Communistic state, seeking escape from the life to which he had been, since his adolescence, committed, but which was really his true life, bound up in the life of Anstey and its owners. He could think now only of the plate cupboard for which he was responsible and could do nothing to protect. He shuffled up towards Rose; she seemed more approachable than Sir Walter, whose aspect was more than usually forbidding.

"My lady," he whispered; "the silver? It will melt."

She turned to him. His concern for their possessions was touching. His whole figure was touching; he looked smaller and older, wrapped, as she had never seen him before, in a brown Jaeger dressing gown with a cord like a monk's round his middle, his feet thrust into a pair of felt slippers of a faded tartan. Out of the dressing-gown pocket protruded the precious shinbone, a little circumstance which moved Rose nearer to tears than she had been moved for years. Was this, then, the only treasure of his own that Summers had thought to snatch up? Perhaps it was the only treasure he had? Even as Svend's collar had been Svend's only possession.

"I'm afraid, Summers," she said gently, "it is not only the silver that will melt. In any case, you must not attempt to go near the house. If we are able to rescue a few things, it can only be under direction; don't you go taking risks."

Annie-housemaid and Mrs. Whiffle, seeing her in conversation with Summers, drew near for comfort, they, also looking very different from their usual selves. Rose gave them a smile of rueful reassurance.

Walter came up to her.

"Look, we can't stand here doing nothing any longer. Dick and Robin and I are going to see if we can get anything out from the back of the house. The fire seems to be mostly in the front; it must have started in the hall or the dining room or my sitting room. You stay here and send Summers round to tell me when the firemen arrive. They ought to be here at any minute. Two of the gardeners have turned up; they will come with me. Understand?"

Her abnormal, excessive fear of violence in any form seized upon her, now that she thought he might be going into danger. So long as she could see him standing in physical safety beneath her eyes, she cared very little what happened to their belongings.

"For pity's sake!" she cried, catching him by the wrist.

Surprised, he paused, and saw the terror in her face.

"Don't worry," he said kindly; "we shan't do anything rash."

"Dick will look after him, Rosie," said Lucy with her feminine acceptance of the man's infallibility.

Still she held him back, imploring.

"Listen," he said, half bothered and half touched by her anxiety, "why don't you and Lucy and Juliet go and sit in the lodge? Take Annie and Mrs. Whiffle with you. There's no point in your staying out here, you will only catch cold."

"Catch cold!" This utterly disproportionate consideration made Rose laugh, even then. "Catch cold, when beams may be falling on your head! It's like Summers telling me that the silver will melt. . . . Listen!" she said, holding up her hand: "Listen: don't you hear something?"

Above the howling of the wind, they heard the clangour of a bell and the tearing scream of a klaxon. Headlights came sweeping in a great fan round the bend of the drive. "Saved!" said Rose, but what she meant was Walter, not Anstey.

ह∾

It seemed hours since she had first aroused him, though in fact not more than an hour had elapsed: the local fire service had arrived with commendable rapidity. The fire, however, abetted by the wind, had got too good a start on them and was now raging through all the windows on the ground floor. The watchers out on the grass could see the interior of the rooms illuminated by that savage glow. The panelling of the hall had caught, and even as they looked they saw the canvas of a portrait give an extra little spurt of a yellower flame and flutter without its frame to the floor. This was the odd thing to observe: the mingling of such small detail and Wagnerian holocaust. Thus, the remnants of the long brocade curtains began to descend in large black flakes all over the grass, to be scurried away again by the wind, scarcely giving them time to alight; like a flock of birds, they rerose upwards to be whirled about the sky. The fate of the curtains seemed to upset Lucy more than anything; unable to grasp the magnitude of the general perdition, here was a thing within her scope, and its comprehensibility seemed to afford her a certain solace, something that she could hold on to and put into words. "Terrible! Terrible!" she had hitherto been muttering to herself as Anstey blazed, but now she came close to Rose as one housewife to another and said:

"Oh, Rosie, those beautiful curtains! Do you remember, we went and chose the material together; we had lunch first and then you took me in your car, we went to Storey's and I was shocked at you paying three pounds a yard, but you wouldn't listen to me; and now look at them. Oh dear, what a pity!"

Pity. That tiny word of two thin syllables, which could mean so much, or, on Lucy's lips, so little. A pity that expensive curtains should be so devoured and wasted. A pity that the crawling millions of mankind should be inspired by no pity for one another. A pity that Anstey should be burning. Pity . . . a pity.

"Lucy!" said Rose. "Do you remember a rhyme I used to say to you in our bedroom after the lights had been put out, to frighten you?

> *"Hitty-pitty within the wall,*
> *Hitty-pitty without the wall.*
> *If you touch Hitty-pitty*
> *Hitty-pitty will bite you."*

Lucy looked at Rose with pity. She thought her sister had momentarily been thrown out of her senses, and no wonder.

"There, there," she said soothingly; "there, there, Rosie. Don't take on so. I daresay it is all meant for the best in the end. God always knows best in the end, doesn't He? We don't know what His purpose may be, do we? We just have to wait and see. I expect they will put the fire out. Men are so very good and brave and clever at that sort of thing. I do feel sorry about the curtains, all the same," she added, "and I do feel sorry for you and Walter, oh dear, I do! How upset I should be if it was Ontibon Street burning, with all our things, Dick's and mine! But God knows best," she repeated; "it may be for the best in the end."

&

Anstey was burning and in no mean measure. Rose realised suddenly that nothing which happened to Walter would ever be on a mean scale. It was another bit of her picture puzzle fitting itself into place. He had arranged his marriage to suit himself in inexorable terms. His professional career had followed a highway of juggernaut triumph. His one and only love, his love for Svend his dog, had ended last night in a most unforeseen form of tragedy. Now his house, his loved Anstey, was burning. There was nothing left to Walter; everything he loved had crashed within these few hours around him. Only his career remained; and Rose supposed that he would continue to make a success of that. It seemed the only thing left to him, now that Svend had gone and Anstey was going.

&

Anstey burnt. It was frightful, and magnificent, to watch the burning. The beauty and terror of the elements, fire and gale savaging this home of civilised man, taking control, making a naught of little man . . . The flames from the house lit up the grass, turning it to a viridescent green, like bad technicolour, and turned the rhododendrons into bushes of unreal technicolour red. It is all unreal, thought Rose; it cannot be true; and yet it is all more

true than anything I have ever known. It is more true to
Walter than anything he has ever known, except the death
of Svend.

&

The burning hulk of Anstey poured out its flames. They
shot a hundred feet into the air, blown by the gale. The
fire had so truly taken hold, that the feeble pressure from
the water mains rendered the hose pipes useless: the thin
jets could do nothing against the wild sheets of flame
streaming outwards and upwards. The men rushed
down to the lake, dragging great lengths of hose through
the daffodils, smashing them down in long reckless
sheaves, and the pump was standing by to siphon the water
up towards the house, but it was already too late; it became
more evident every moment that the house would go.
Smoke was beginning to issue through the tiles of the roof,
and was pouring out through the chimneys, smoke tongued
with scarlet, seized by the wind and whirled away, mad
grey hair becoming entangled in treetops; and the sky
overhead turned ruddy, so that people who had heard the
siren and looked out of their windows to see where the fire
might be, saw it from miles off. There was a continuous
roar, stitched through with crackling, and the heat was
now so intense that the watchers, feeling their faces scorch,
retreated ever further and further in silent little groups as
though abashed before the wrath of God. The water from
the lake had begun to flow, but although the stream from
the big pipe was powerful it affected the furnace not at all,
save that a fierce hissing was now added to the roar. The
figures of the firemen ran hither and thither, shouting,

hauling, like small demons in a frescoed portrayal of Hell. Shoals of huge red sparks eddied across the night, excelling any fireflies in size and brilliance. They alighted sometimes on the clothes of the watchers, to be brushed irritably aside, but for the most part they streamed away in flight until suddenly and blackly extinguished.

ࢠ

The roof was the first thing to give way. They saw it sag, as the fire reached the battens and gratefully ate them up in welcome tinder, dry and sere after two centuries and more. The battens of Queen Anne's day, as dead as she. They saw it sag, curtseying in little dips of surrender to a dominating power. They heard, through the roar and the hissing, the sound of tiles falling, some sliding down to break themselves in a brittle death on the terrace, others coming down in their massed thousands, right through the house, to a more thunderous death on what had once been the floor of the hall, the dining room, Walter's sitting room. The great collapse of the roof had some nobility about it, unlike the small attempt at self-saving of the tiles that had slid off separately and alone; "Yet," thought Rose, standing out there in a confusion of mind she had had no chance or time to organise, "I honour the little tile that has found its own way to the ground, smashed itself, and refused to come down with the multitude."

ࢠ

By five o'clock in the morning, dawn arrived, a grey dawn. The burning house took the place of the invisible sun, in a sunrise redder than any shepherd's warning. It was then that the internal work of destruction, eating away, began to show its effect. A warning cry of "Stand back!" made the firemen leap aside. The watchers, in their ignorance, stood wondering what could be about to happen, when in dismay they saw the pediment over the hall door begin to waver and finally crash forward into ruin on the little terrace at the top of the steps. "Just where Svend always lay!" thought Rose. "Waiting for Walter to come home."

That first crash of the pediment came as the precursor of others. The fall of Anstey went quickly, once it had begun. Undermined, the masonry must crumble. That the pediment should collapse might be a slight thing, the loss of an inessential feature, but now the whole wall of the front must follow, exposing the rooms within. Little as yet could be discerned through the gaping windows, for although the flames were dying down for lack of wood to feed on, the smoke still rose in obscuring billows. Bit by bit the final breaking up started: what was so shocking about it, was that the watchers saw no sign of disintegration until the violent event occurred; then, a piece of wall tumbled forward, and then another, and then another, lump by lump, crashing in noisy heaps of scattering brick on the terrace, Anstey no longer Anstey but a broken thing, resolved by violence into its constituent parts, no longer a unity but a hideous, charred, smoking caricature of its distinction, graciousness, and elegance.

෨෨

To the inexperienced eye it seemed incredible that solid structure should so completely dissolve. Phrases such as "safe as houses" or "the roof over our heads" came into the mind, to be instantly negatived by the spectacle presented. By the time the whole façade had toppled, and lay in amorphous masses of brick, plaster, and rubble, either on the terrace or piling up inside, where the ground floor rooms had once been, there was no more left than a foundation half the height of a man, running the length of what had been the house. It was possible to see right inside, into the shell where only some fragments of party walls remained, reminders of the shapes of the rooms. The staircase had vanished, and so had the floors dividing the upper storey from the ground floor; the timber of the joists and girders had been consumed. All was empty, save for some floating trails of smoke. Naked and uncovered, all those ghosts of the familiar rooms: the bedrooms upstairs, the hall below, the dining room, Walter's sitting room, less familiar now, a mere anatomy, stripped of their comfort, of their furniture, and of the pretty panelling which once had graced that stark, blackened brickwork beneath.

All splendour had departed. The rarefied air of the tragic plane can seldom be breathed beyond a few hours. Some counteraction comes to relieve the strain, even though it may come in the form of bathos, absurdity, or squalor. Anstey, so grandly burning: now went out. Fire may be a terrible thing, but the petering out of fire is worse. It is a mean ending of life; it has not even the positive nobility of death; it is a smouldering.

The flames had now subsided, and only a few little snakes of fire flickered their tongues here and there, instantly damped out of existence by a fireman running around, dragging a pipe, and squirting a jet with a hiss on to the threatened revival. The firemen themselves had lost their semblance of small demons running amongst the fires of Hell, and had now resolved themselves into local characters such as the chemist and the butcher and the youth who delivered groceries on Tuesday mornings. The few flames that still tried to keep their little life going paled with the coming of daylight; they lost their glow; the grand contrast of red flame on black night was over. There had been a magnificence in ruin; now there was nothing but a dying stench of wet and charred remains.

Chapter 12.

TUESDAY MORNING

The only part of Anstey that had been saved was the servants' wing at the back. Summers herded them all into his pantry with some pride, as though he might take credit to himself for the preservation of this habitable room. He brought chairs in from the kitchen, ranged them round the table, dusted them, and invited his guests to make themselves at home. Exhausted, they sank down; they scarcely spoke; Lucy furtively reached out for the squeeze of Dick's comforting hand; Juliet began to search in her handbag for lipstick and powder.

"We all look so frightful, darlings," she said. "Hadn't we better do something about it?"

These, the first practical words spoken for many hours,

restored some kind of sanity. Rose even laughed, looking at Juliet with grateful affection. Lucy, she knew, would ask no better than to indulge in an emotional scene, with tears, sympathy, and huggings. Far better that Lucy should be told to powder her nose.

They did, indeed, all look frightful. Rose herself, although she was unaware of it, had a black smudge across her chin. Juliet without make-up was a travesty of the lovely Lady Quarles. Lucy was all to bits, in her old rain-coat, her figure bulging out in the fleshy places because she had not had time to put on the controlling under-clothes. The men showed less signs of difference—save for a slight growth of beard: Robin had smoothed back his hair with the palms of his hands into its crisp wavy close-ness, and Dick looked much as usual, pink and jovial, ready to make a joke whenever he thought Rose and Walter would be in the mood to accept it.

Walter was not there. He was out talking to the fire-brigade men; he would come in presently. Rose wondered how she had best meet him, when they were left alone together, in private. What should she say, or leave unsaid? Svend. Anstey. There was so much to be said, and even more to be left unspoken. All her knowledge of Walter, all her love, all her tact, would now be gathered up into a supreme demand.

"Here, Lucy," said Juliet. "I simply can't go on calling you Mrs. Packington, do you mind? Here's the powder, take it; help yourself."

She handed it over, across the pantry table. Lucy accepted it, pleased, but as gingerly as someone accepting a pernicious drug.

಄

Summers in his Jaeger dressing gown had disappeared into the kitchen, where he and Mrs. Whiffle and Annie-housemaid were trying to prepare some breakfast. The French cook from London had long since taken refuge in a gardener's cottage, saying *"Moi, je n'aime pas ce geure d'embêtements-là, ce n'est pas pour cela que je me suis engagé chez Sir Mortibois et sa lady; j'espère bien qu'ils vont me compenser de tout ce que j'ai perdu; sinon, j'aurai recours à mon homme d'affaires."* Summers, meanwhile, was boiling eggs and making tea and setting out everything as best he could to make it look like breakfast in the dining room. He bustled about, fetching silver spoons and knives from his plate cupboard in the pantry, laying them on the table, bustling back into the kitchen to make sure that Mrs. Whiffle was not letting the eggs boil for more than three minutes. He had taken his white pantry apron down from its hook on the door and was now wearing it with most incongruous effect over his dressing gown.

"Summers," said Rose, getting up, struck with remorse, "you must be quite as tired as we are; let us come and help."

It was a relief to have something to do, and when Dick dropped a cup they were all foolishly amused, except for Summers who clapped his hands over his mouth and was heard to murmur, "I shouldn't have brought out the best Crown Derby."

ह॰

"What time is it?" said Lucy suddenly.

None of them had a watch, but the pantry clock was still ticking away, a moonfaced metal-rimmed object propped on tiny legs. Five minutes to nine.

"It can't be!" said Rose.

"My lady, in thirty years I have never known him gain more than a quarter of an hour in the week. I correct him regular, and when I am not here Mrs. Whiffle obliges for me."

"Oh, Dick, what *will* they be thinking at the office? You have never been late before."

Dick looked guilty: he had forgotten all about the office.

"Better telephone," he said, looking round for the instrument.

There it stood, uncompromisingly black in a corner of the window sill.

"Dead," he said, holding the receiver to his ear, "dead as mutton." He put the receiver back. "Can't be helped," he said. "I've got a good excuse, anyway—better than the office boy's grandmother's funeral. Ha, ha—what?" His large smile beamed round: he had placed his joke.

"All the same," said Rose, seeing Lucy's worried face, "you ought to let them know. We could send Johnson down with a telegram to the village. And you, Juliet, I expect you had appointments for today which you would like to alter. We had better write out a whole flock of telegrams and send Johnson with them. The garage hasn't been burnt, so the motorcars must still be there. And Walter," she said; "I don't know what engagements Walter had for today; perhaps he also will want to send telegrams. . . . I wonder where he is?" she said. "Robin, would you go and look for him and tell him his breakfast is getting cold? Tell him to come in and eat it and keep the firemen and the police waiting for a bit."

Robin went thankfully into escape.

Summers came forward.

"My lady, and Mr. Packington, sir; if I might suggest?
. . . The wireless . . . They give a news bulletin at
9 A.M. on the Light Programme I listen to it always while
I am cleaning the plate. . . . If I might suggest that we
should now turn it on? It will certainly mention the trouble that has come on us: I saw a number of press represent-
atives arriving in cars, with notebooks. The news must
have reached London by now, my lady: you know what the
press is."

"Yes, Summers," said Rose; "I know what the press is,
but I doubt if a fire at Anstey would get into the news. And
anyway, the electricity has gone, so the wireless won't
work."

"Mine is a battery set," said Summers, switching it on.
It roared out in a cacophony of saxophones from some
foreign station. After a little adjustment, a voice said, "This
is the BBC Light Programme. Here is the news."

Then followed the usual depressing headlines, but Summers had been right: the conclusion came. "The manor
house of Anstey, the residence of Sir Walter Mortibois,
Q.C., noted for its landscape gardens, was totally destroyed
by fire during the night. No lives were lost, or injuries
sustained."

"Now everyone will know," said Summers with some
satisfaction. "Word will go round."

ह●

They began to talk in a subdued way. The thought of
Walter was uppermost in all their minds, but even Lucy

felt it would be better to refrain from mentioning him. Every time a sound came from outside they looked at the door, thinking he might be about to enter. He was the smitten man.

They talked in little jerky phrases, mostly about their immediate plans. Rose detected in herself an apologetic attitude, as though by her own fault she had brought inconvenience upon them, saying that Johnson should drive them all up to London as soon as things could be organised; she had her own car here, she said, so Johnson and the big car could easily be spared. Dick saw his opportunity and pounced.

"Well, it won't take us long to pack," he said heartily. "That's one good thing."

"Oh, Dick!" said Lucy, who had been trying very hard not to think of their poor lost possessions. How on earth were they to be replaced, with things the price they were? She really had tried not to think; it seemed mean when Rose and Walter had lost so much more; but of course she had packed all their best things to bring to Anstey—Dick's two new shirts and her own best coat and skirt, and many little treasures such as Dick's evening cigarette case and his leather stud box, and the handkerchiefs with his initials. Dick, for his part, was thinking about his golf clubs: he had bought himself a new canvas bag for the occasion and half a dozen new balls.

Rose, coming to her senses with a shock of remorse, laid her hand on her sister's. Delicacy of feeling prevented her from saying that she and Walter would make good any losses; so she put it more tactfully:

"Luce, you do realise that everything is covered by insurance, don't you?"

"Oh, I wasn't thinking of *that*," said Lucy mendaciously. "I was just thinking how odd we shall all look, arriving in London like this—no hats or gloves, and these old coats; I think it's rather funny, really I do."

"I feel rather ashamed of having grabbed my fur coat," said Juliet. "It was the first thing I could find."

"Did you take your pearls, Juliet?"

"I had them on. Look."

She pulled them out from under her jersey.

"Do you always sleep in them? I thought it was supposed to be bad for pearls."

"One person tells you one thing, and another another. So I just keep them on and let them take their chance."

"They say some people are bad for pearls," said Lucy, "and other people can bring them back to life. Do you think that's true?"

"They say the way you can tell real pearls from false is that real pearls don't crumble even if you drive the wheels of a farm cart over them," said Dick. "I don't know if there's anything in it. Do you know, Rose?"

"No," said Rose; "no, I don't know if there's anything in it. Those Japanese cultured pearls, for instance . . ."

ॐ

Walter came in, followed by Robin. They were both dirty, their hands blackened, their faces smeared. Rose had never seen Walter in so disreputable a disarray, he was always so neatly grey, so well shaven, well brushed, and kempt. She was at a loss to know how to greet this tramplike

Walter; so much lay behind their meeting, it would take months to straighten it out. There was the thing that only she and Walter knew, about Svend, and there was now this other thing which everyone knew, the destruction of Anstey. The private and the public griefs. The peculiar terms of their marriage made it hard for her to deal with so unforeseen a situation; yet it corresponded to the fear that had always shadowed her, the fear of violence, the fear of sorrow, how should she meet it, if it came? It corresponded also to the shyness she had never overcome with Walter: how naturally and spontaneously, she thought with sudden envy, would Lucy have rushed to Dick!

Juliet, quick to sense another woman's predicament, burst in with one of her reckless remarks, which sounded wrong but which was in fact infallibly right.

"Oh, Walter darling!" she said. "I've known you for many years now, but I never believed you could look *funny.*"

Lucy was horrified by such levity. She saved it up in her mind to discuss with Dick later on, when they should have struggled back to the safeness and security of Ontibon Street, and there would be such an exciting wealth of things to discuss, enough to feed Lucy's speculative chatter for the next ten years. "Do you remember? . . ." she would say. And then there would be something about, "Do you remember how rude that brazen Lady Quarles was to poor Walter when he came into the pantry on that awful morning, poor man, with his face dirty? I would have pretended not to notice. I saw that poor Rosie didn't know what to say. How right I was in thinking there was something between Walter and Juliet—I suppose I may call her

Juliet, as she called me Lucy. No woman would dare to speak to a man in the way she spoke to Walter unless—— Well, Pudding, you know what I mean."

It would be comfortable to be able to call Dick Pudding again at home, without any second thoughts.

"Yes, Pood," he would say, "I expect you're right. Wise little woman. I never did trust that Lady Quarles."

ह&

To Rose's surprise, Walter did not look in the least downcast. He looked cheerful and even amused. Adversity seemed to have rejuvenated him; or perhaps it was partly due to his incongruously comic appearance. He was carrying a small bundle wrapped in a piece of sacking, which he deposited beside the dead telephone.

"Don't touch it," he said, "it's hot. Summers, can Mr. Robin and I have a wash in your sink? I haven't seen my own face, but, judging by Mr. Robin's, I expect we both need it. Are the taps working or have the pipes melted at the main?"

A trickle of water came through. Walter sluiced his head vigorously, with as much enjoyment as a young man at a mountain stream. Summers looked on in consternation: never had he thought to see Sir Walter bending over the pantry sink, and the water not even warm. He hurried forward with a towel from his cupboard.

"If you and Mr. Robin and Mr. Packington would care to borrow my razor . . ." he said. "I have a packet of new blades . . . I keep the outfit in here, for I sometimes find it necessary to shave a second time in the day before serving dinner, and I have not always time to go up to my bedroom, especially when the weather is warm. It is a safety razor, Sir Walter, same as your own. You will find it quite customary to use."

"Go on, Walter," said Juliet. "Accept Summers' offer. I've never yet been privileged to watch you shave; it will be a new experience."

"One lives and learns, doesn't one?" said Dick, pleased to find this phrase to summarise the events of the past few hours.

Lucy felt and looked stiff disapproval. It was all right and natural for Walter to wash and shave with Rose looking on, and all right and natural for Dick and even Robin to wash and shave with Lucy looking on; but to do it in front of Lady Quarles, whom she was now, apparently, authorised to address as Juliet, came as an outrage of propriety. There could be only one interpretation, the interpretation Lucy had already set in her own mind on the relationship between Juliet and Walter. They had spent passionate nights together—poor deceived Rosie!—And that teasing, mischievous way in which Juliet had said, "I've never yet been privileged to watch you shave," meant that they had always parted before dawn, in the romantic hour, before men's chins begin to grow a prickly stubble and women cease to look their best. Juliet and Walter, in their elegance and distinction, would always have avoided the necessary repair in front of one another. It had never hitherto occurred to Lucy that that might mark the difference between romance and marriage; another thought to be put away for future consideration.

Then, joining up with Dick's last remark, she said, "Yes, indeed! One lives *and* learns, doesn't one? There are so many things, aren't there, that one had never thought about?"

&❧

Walter turned round, his face lathered, to grin at Rose and Juliet, taking them into his confidence as allies in the opposite camp to Lucy and Dick. Robin, waiting for his turn to wash, still blackened and dirty, got included in the grin, a complicity which flattered him beyond all the dreams of the distant cult he had been building up round his uncle Walter since Friday evening. He thought now that his uncle Walter gave him a special wink meant exclusively for himself; perhaps he imagined it; perhaps Uncle Walter had never noticed him at all. . . .

Lady Quarles treated Walter with no respect.

"You look like a clown," she said, "with a puff of Summers' shaving soap on the end of your nose. Wipe it off, Walter, and sit down to eat your egg in the ordinary way, like a man having his breakfast. Rose, you don't mind my ordering your husband about, do you? We are all in such a mess it doesn't seem to matter what anyone does or what anyone says. Perhaps that is the way one ought always to live, only it seems a pity to have to burn the house down in order to realise it. Rose, do tell Walter to sit down and eat that egg and drink that coffee; then he can tell us what he has got in that little bundle he put down by the telephone and warned us it was too hot to touch."

"Dear Juliet!" thought Rose. "She dashes in with her nonsense mixed with sense. Dear Juliet, she is trying to help me out. She is helping both me and Walter, her friends; yet Walter, for some inexplicable reason, does not seem in need of help; he seems to be sustained on an up-lifting wave."

"I have spent a really interesting hour with the firemen," Walter said. "One has no idea what peculiar things can happen. Now, for instance, there is a greenfinch's nest in the ceanothus of the west wall of my room, and the bird is still quietly sitting. Unbelievable, I should have said. Another extraordinary thing: a scuttle full of coals has fallen right through from the top of the house—I recognised it as the one from your bedroom, Rose—and has come to rest in what was the hall. It has not overturned, and the coals have not burnt."

"They must have been very bad coals," said Lucy seriously.

"Then there is this," said Walter, cautiously unwrapping his little bundle. "One of the men found it and brought it to me. Look, it is one of those Wedgwood urns that used to stand on the mantelpiece in the hall; it is not even chipped, and it has become entirely coated in molten glass. See, it is intact inside its transparent covering; you can see the pattern and the colours."

"A real curiosity," said Lucy.

"Our only surviving ornament," said Walter. "I think I shall use it as a mascot to take into court with me. Unless Rose wants it?"

"Walter, I do think you are wonderful," said Juliet; "the way you take it all."

"Isn't it lucky Svend wasn't here?" said Lucy. "He would have been frightened out of his life. Animals are terrified of fire. One has heard awful stories of trapped horses screaming."

"Lucy," said Rose hastily, "are you sure you have had enough breakfast? I can't begin to tell you all what I feel about this—your things burnt, and so on. Luce, you had better come to luncheon with me tomorrow, and we'll go shopping."

"Lovely!" said Lucy, and never had she spoken more sincerely. Rose needed managing in shops, for she always seemed oddly nervous with the assistants, but she was generous, even to a shocking degree.

"Meanwhile," said Juliet, "we ought to leave these poor people, don't you think? They must want to collect their wits, and I am sure they feel their Easter party has lasted quite long enough."

ह∾

Johnson could not bring the car round to the front since the drive was filled with hills of smoking debris; so his passengers, Lady Quarles, Mr. and Mrs. Packington, and Mr. Robin, all came round to the stable yard, where the garage was, and got in there. Rose and Walter came to see them off. It was an odd departure for their party. Lucy was frankly crying; and for the first time Rose felt the tears pricking at her own eyes. She was also a little apprehensive of being left alone with Walter, but after the car had driven away and they had waved a final farewell he put his hand through her arm in a most unaccustomed gesture and turned to pace with her in an easy and friendly way. She looked up; he was smiling down at her.

"Well, my dear," he said, "there seems little left for us to do but to contemplate the ruins of our home."

She could not trust herself to make anything but practical remarks.

"I suppose we must think about getting back to London. There seems no point in remaining here. Will you come with me in my car? Johnson is coming back to collect the servants. They will have their luggage. I don't think they have lost anything unless some water has got in through the roof and done any damage."

"No, their rooms are all right; I have been up to see. The police will put a guard over that wing. Mrs. Whiffle will be here during the day time, and will go home to sleep at her mother's in the village. She doesn't fancy the idea of sleeping here alone at night."

"I don't blame her, poor woman. What time is it, Walter?"

"No watch," he said. "Judging by the sun, it must be about midday. We shall never again hear the clock strike!"

"Walter, *don't* . . . Have you thought at all of what you will do? Attempt to rebuild?"

"We should never get a licence. I thought we might move into the servants' wing. Just you and I; no guests. We could picnic, couldn't we, at week ends, with only Mrs. Whiffle? Should you mind?"

"Mind!" The whole of life seemed to be altering for her.

"After all," he continued, "we have got the garden left, and I think that was what we both cared most about at Anstey. Neither of us set much store by a large house and parties."

"Walter, darling," she said. "I love you, you know."

"I know," he said. "Bless you. Bless you for loving me and for being so understanding."

The soft ghost of Svend trotted past them, but neither of them made any reference.

"Look," said Walter, changing his tone, "I shall have to go and have some last words with the police, but before I go I want to show you something. I don't think I have ever been more touched in my life. I've been given a present. An Easter present."

"A present?"

"Yes. To make up for the loss of Anstey."

He took from his pocket the shinbone of the stag and held it out to her.

"Oh, Walter! . . . Summers?"

"Summers. He asked if I would do him the favour of accepting it."

This time tears did really come into Rose's eyes; he saw them.

"I must go now," he said; "I expect the constable is waiting for me. When would you like to start? In about an hour?"

"I'll get the car out," she said.

❧

Walter gone, she made her way slowly towards the stable yard. She knew that there was a crowd of people out on the front, villagers gaping at the still-smouldering ruins. "Don't it smell nasty?" they were saying, sniffing the wet, charred wood, taking a sadistic pleasure in outrage. But the police were keeping them back, and she could count on being alone. She badly wanted a few minutes to herself; never had she wanted them more; and it was with annoyance that she heard a motor horn just round the corner. In the circumstances, however, anything was to be expected; it might be the insurance people come to inspect; it might be a press car; it might be anybody.

It was Gilbert.

He came hurrying on foot, having left his car out of sight.

"Rose!"

"Gilbert! How good of you! You had heard?"

"It was on the wireless. My man told me. I came as soon as I could. You are all right? Where is Walter? Where are the others?"

"The others have gone back to London. You must have passed them on the road. Walter is talking to the police. How glad he will be to see you!"

"He will be gladder than you know. Rose, I can't tell you what a beast I feel, what an utter beast. Poor Walter, I put too much upon him; too much for one day. But how could I foresee this?"

"You couldn't," said Rose gravely. "You are thinking of Svend, of course. You mustn't blame yourself; it is just terribly unfortunate. You couldn't know."

"Rose, did you really believe I would take his dog from him?"

"You did take him."

"But I have brought him back."

"Brought him back? Alive?"

"Alive, and as well as ever he was."

"I don't understand—— Oh, I see. You heard the news of the fire at nine; you hadn't had time to begin your . . . your horrible butchery."

"Rose, you misjudge me. I swear I never had the slightest intention of laying a finger upon him."

She stared at Gilbert.

"I understand less and less."

"Let us say that I thought Walter needed a lesson, both for his own sake and for yours," he said slowly. "Shall we leave it at that? Miracles don't happen, but I thought it might make a difference. I palmed off a lot of nonsense on Walter, which the youngest medical student would have seen through, but, coming from me, he accepted it. I nearly convinced him; then at the last moment he put up a final struggle, and refused. So I had to invent a further tarradiddle, something to do with Svend's eyes—all quite untrue—but it worked, and there you are."

There was a long pause, of the sort that becomes inevitable when people have so large a background of things to say that they had better be left unsaid. Rose could not now survey the past, nor form any estimate of Gilbert's wisdom; she could grasp only, and that with a blundering difficulty, the events of the last two days.

"But you telephoned, Gilbert," she said, groping into her memory. "You took Svend away on Sunday evening before dinner. Then you telephoned to Walter to say it was all over. He told me. He said it was good of you to let him know, meaning, I suppose, that it was considerate of you not to keep him in suspense longer than necessary. You must forgive me, Gilbert, if I get a bit confused about the times that different things have happened these last few days. . . . Why did you ring up Walter, to say it was all over? It was cruel of you. The whole thing has been cruel from beginning to end."

"I know," said Gilbert. "I intended it to be cruel. That telephone message was the last twisting of the screws that stretched Walter on the rack. I wanted him to know what suffering could be."

"You would have spared me a great deal, if you had let me into your secret."

"Dear Rose, if you had known the truth, you would never have kept it to yourself. You could not have endured to watch Walter's misery."

She smiled at last.

"I suppose I must forgive you. In the meantime, where have you left Svend?"

"In my car. Wait there," said Gilbert, going off.

She heard the car door shut as Svend came questing round the corner.

"Svend," she said, "where's Walter? Find Walter!"